He Is Not Gone

He Is Not Gone

Bernard Brunsting

ZONDERVAN
PUBLISHING HOUSE

OF THE ZONDERVAN CORPORATION | GRAND RAPIDS, MICHIGAN 49506

HE IS NOT GONE

© 1961 by Bernard Brunsting.

Sixth printing 1978

Library of Congress
Catalog Card Number: 74-29696
ISBN 0-310-22052-1

Printed in the United States of America

To my wife
ALICE

It was my privilege to meet Danny and his wonderfully dedicated Christian parents, and I shall never forget the experience. Though short, little Danny's life had spiritual magnitude. Certainly the story of Danny and his parents' fight with leukemia is a victorious, though sad, one and leaves no doubt of Christian triumph over suffering.

May God bless the author and readers with a stimulating and fresh awareness of the power of our Lord Jesus Christ.

DALE EVANS ROGERS

Chapter I

On Friday, November 14, I took our three-year-old son Danny to see the doctor. The evening before I had called Dr. Martin at his home to talk about Danny. He was out, but I did speak with his wife and explained to her our concern. I told her, "For some time now we've noticed that Danny has difficulty in walking. He walks like an old man who has arthritis or rheumatism." She said she would tell her husband.

We had first noticed Danny's difficulty several weeks before, just after we got him new orthopedic shoes. He had flat feet like his dad, so we attributed his shuffle to his new shoes. There were no other indications of illness. His appetite and spirit were fine. But gradually the shuffle grew worse until it was almost impossible for him to walk.

That Friday morning Dr. Martin gave him a careful examination. He asked me several questions which led me to understand that he was gravely concerned. After the examination I asked him what he thought. He said, "Danny needs a more thorough examination than can be given in a private office. I'll make an appointment for you at Children's Hospital in Hollywood."

"Doctor," I said, "just what do you have in mind?"

His reply was, "There are many things which are possible."

"Like what?" I asked.

"For one thing he said, "I am thinking of muscular dystrophy."

This struck me like a blow, and I suspected we were in for real trouble.

We had faced trouble before. In the summer of 1949 when we had three children (two were born later), all three were in the hospital at one time with polio. When I heard Dr. Martin's words, the same sickening feeling I had known that summer returned. I remembered how that matter had been committed to the Lord and how He gave relief. Even though one of our children, Bernie, was permanently handicapped by the disease, God had given us a permanent relief. This, too, must be committed to Him.

The Sunday evening before, I had preached on the subject "Jesus, the Man of Prayer" at the Parkview Church in Santa Ana. It was the fifth and final service of a week of special meetings which we had called "The School of Prayer." Among other things I said in that Sunday evening service was this: "In Mark 14:33 it tells us that Jesus was 'sore amazed, and . . . very heavy.' This means that the point where self-control would be lost was near, and that to be pushed just a bit further would mean plunging into chaos and panic." One of the points of my message was that Jesus prayed the prayer of submission when He said, "Thy will be done." This prayer was made when He was "sore amazed" and "very heavy" — that is, near the point of panic. I pointed out that He did not cry, "Oh, God, spare me!" In John 12:27 these words of Jesus are recorded: "Now is my soul troubled; and what shall I say? Father, save me from this hour. . . ." No, He would not say that. He would say instead, "Thy will be done." All this I had said in a somewhat detached, abstract way. But before the week was finished, I began to know the testing of submission.

When Danny and I came from the doctor's office, my wife Alice was in the kitchen. Alice and I had always been honest with each other. We had tried to face reality. We had been through too much together to make any change. I told her, "Honey, it doesn't look very good." I think both of us had an undeclared premonition; now it had been verbalized. For a moment we cried together. We would do so again and again in the next few days.

On Saturday, according to a previous promise, I took our oldest child Al to the Annual Auto Show. A friend of his and several of mine went with us. One of these friends was Bob Honig, a member of the church and a close personal friend. I had shared with him our concern for

Danny. In the midst of all the glitter and dazzle of the "Biggest Auto Show on Earth," I made two remarks to Bob. At one point I said, "You know, Bob, when a person has a concern such as ours, he may make a comment or two about these cars, he may respond with laughter to a humorous remark, but all this is very much on the surface. Inside, in the real person, it is a much different picture." How often a smile or a blithe word covers a deep sorrow or hidden fear.

The other remark I made to Bob was about the relative value of things in life. At the show we saw a Rolls Royce, a Lincoln Continental, and other expensive autos. But at that moment the health of one little boy was of more value to me than all the cars in the world. How ridiculously unimportant the externals of life become when the heart is torn in two. How trivial are the luxuries of the world when the soul is disquieted within. Our scale of values is altered when the larger burdens of life come.

The next Sunday was a difficult day. We still did not know what was wrong with Danny, but we were aware that it could be something extremely serious. At the evening service my eyes welled with tears, and I had to fight for control of my voice. Danny was weaker. Besides having difficulty in walking, his back hurt him, especially when he coughed, and I had noticed an unexplained bruise on his arm. For the first time there flickered into my mind the possibility of leukemia.

On Monday morning I called Children's Hospital to find out when we could take Danny in for a checkup. The receptionist told me, "We will notify you by mail when you can come in." We called our family doctor and told him and asked if there weren't some way to get Danny in sooner. He suggested a specialist to us. The next afternoon we took Danny to a pediatrician. He made a thorough examination and sent us to a medical laboratory where a blood smear was made. Within an hour he made his diagnosis and called. First he talked to Alice and told her that the trouble had been located in the blood stream and that Danny was anemic. Then he asked to talk with me.

"Reverend Brunsting," he said, "I told your wife that Danny is anemic. I want to give you the full picture — your son has leukemia."

Those were the hardest words I had ever heard in my life. As I held my wife and shared them with her, our faces flooded with tears; the meaning of those words began to become real to us.

Besides being involved in the sorrow of death as a pastor, I had faced death three times previously in a very personal way. Once in college when a close friend was killed in an automobile accident when I was driving. Again, when my brother, a pilot of a B-17 bomber in World War II, was shot out of the skies over enemy territory. And finally, when my father, at the age of fifty-five, suddenly died from a heart attack. Now again I was seeing death face to face. The "inevitable rendezvous" was frightening. How does one face it? We had to learn.

Much is done to minister to the physical needs of sick children. Trained nurses on twenty-four-hour duty, a staff of doctors, and the best medical facilities in the world are all employed in their behalf. Anything at all would be done to give them help. But what of the families? They, too, have a real need — a need that cannot be fulfilled by medicines, drugs, or doctors. We needed such help, and we found it. It was in the prayers and love expressed by loved ones.

The writer of Hebrews (12:1) expressed our feelings when he wrote: "Wherefore seeing we also are compassed about with so great a cloud of witnesses . . . ." We were beginning to feel we were "compassed about" with the loving care and prayers of "a cloud" of friends. What a rich and deep joy it is to belong to "the family of God." Nothing touches one without it being a concern of all. One helps the other, and together the experiences of life are met. Even if personal and eternal salvation were excluded, just to belong to God's family for the here and now would be eminently worthwhile. When we recite the Apostle's Creed and come to the words, "I believe in . . . the communion of saints," they live with a meaning never before realized.

On Wednesday morning Danny was admitted to Children's Hospital on Sunset Boulevard in Hollywood. Here in the heart of the film and TV capital of the world we found warmth of heart and skill of hand not usually associated with this world of pretense. The staff of doctors from the Hematology Department see as many cases of leukemia as any men in the world. To these scientific experts, no one is a "case" — each is a person. The parents are people with whom they talk. There is warmth and feeling, and both are important. Medicines relieve and cure disease, but there are no pills or drugs for the depressed and wounded spirit of man. Our day of specialization and science needs the warm meeting of heart to heart. Man is not an unfeeling machine. He is flesh and feeling.

One day I noticed this little sign on the nurses' bulletin board in the hospital:

To handle yourself use your head;
To handle others use your heart.

When the head and the heart are used for others, men and women become fully available in the service of God to humanity. Either without the other is incomplete.

While Danny's mother went with the nurse to take him to his room, I stayed in the admitting office to make the necessary financial arrangements and fill out the forms. When I had finished, I was told I could join my wife. For a moment I went in the room with her and Danny, but my heart was so filled I had to leave. In the brief moment I was there, however, I realized that it would not be hard for him to stay. I mentioned to him, "Danny, this will be just like a vacation trip for you."

"Yeah," he said, "this is like a motel, isn't it, daddy?" Then another advantage occurred to him, "And I get to stay here and Dorothy doesn't." Dorothy, his sister, was two years older than Danny, but they were inseparable companions, often competing with each other; to have something that she didn't seemed all right to him.

Now we were beginning to ask ourselves the inevitable question, "Why?" At one point I said to Alice, "It seems to me it would be far better if Danny had never been born than to have him a few years and lose him." If he had never come into the world, there would never be pain for him or sorrow for us. Yet, surely, that could not be the right attitude. If God had brought Danny into the world only as a plaything for us and then snatched him back again after a brief time it would be a cruel and senseless thing. But God is neither cruel nor senseless. There must be a purpose, and this purpose must come to light and definition. We asked God to show us, and gradually He led us into the mysteries of His ways.

On Thursday morning we received a helpful visit from two ministerial friends Floyd Goulouze and Ed Hibma. What was particularly significant about their visit was that before this I had talked with Alice and the doctor about Danny but had not yet talked with anyone else because I knew I would go to pieces. Now these two friends came over, and as I talked and sobbed I learned to speak of Danny's illness without breaking down. Floyd and Ed were the ones who went through this ordeal with me, and I am grateful to them for it.

I remember their prayers: Floyd graciously mentioned the tears of the Lord when He was here on earth and said that our tears were not something to be ashamed of, but something we shared with Him. Ed prayed that the scientific progress to find a cure for leukemia might be rapid enough to include Danny.

The Salk vaccine for polio had come too late for our children; maybe the help for leukemia would be found in time. "Is this a possibility?" we asked ourselves. The medical world was working hard at it. Ken Baird, whose little daughter was in the UCLA hospital before her death following a heart operation, said that the doctors there had told him they were very near a "breakthrough" for leukemia. Another friend told us that she knew of someone in the research laboratories at the City of Hope, the well-known cancer hospital in Los Angeles, who had said that such a possibility existed within the next year.

When Alice and I discussed this, she said, "We so much wanted another son, and we love him so dearly that nothing could be more wonderful." We agreed, however, that we had already surrendered our child and that was the way it would stand unless He showed us something different.

On Friday afternoon Dr. Farthing told us the results of the tests were available and that she would talk with us after visiting hours. At 3:30 we met with her, and she introduced us to Dr. Albo of the Hematology Department.

Dr. Albo asked us, "What were you told when you brought your child to us?"

"We were told he has leukemia," I said.

"I must confirm that diagnosis. We have made bone marrow tests, and there is no question about it." Then he went on to explain several things to us which were to prove helpful. His explanations were made in nontechnical language, and we appreciated this.

In the first place, he explained that childhood leukemia is a "universally fatal disease"; medical science knows of no cure. Leukemia is a disease of the blood. The bone marrow, where the body makes its blood, becomes diseased so that it manufactures leukemia (false white) cells and does not have room for the making of red blood cells, true white blood cells, and platelets (the blood coagulator).

He also told us that at that time there were three drugs that were effective in the control of the disease. Each had an effective period of about three months. During this period, called remission, the drug would allow normal production of blood cells in the bone marrow, and the child would return to a normal, active life. During remission children could play, go to school, and in every way live a normal life.

He told us that because leukemia receives much publicity it is well known; nevertheless it is a rare disease. The average doctor never sees a case in a lifetime of practice. "At Children's Hospital," he said, "we probably see as many cases as anywhere in the world, and only fifty cases are admitted here a year from a population area of five and a half million." The doctor also told us that because Children's Hospital sees so many cases, if anything new were developed they would know about it as soon as anybody. In other words, it would be futile to run around the country to try to give Danny the advantage of something "new" we might hear about.

We were also told that using the drugs to gain remission was valuable from two standpoints other than having Danny with us for an additional nine months to a year.* In the first place, during the period of remission it could be possible that a fourth effective drug might be found. I also thought to myself that the extension might produce the cure. The other value was that the misery of the final illness would be shorter than if the drugs were not used.

Another point the doctor mentioned was that we undoubtedly would hear of people who had lived ten or fifteen years with leukemia. (We already had.) But, he explained, this adult leukemia was entirely different from childhood leukemia.

We disagreed with the doctor at one point. He said it would be best not to tell anyone what was wrong because Danny needed to be treated normally and wouldn't be if others knew he had leukemia. This made sense, all right, but we decided we would share what we knew with others. Our main reason for doing this was because we belonged to a family, the family of God, and families share their joys and sorrows with each other. It was true that some might be inclined to treat Danny differently, but this could be avoided by explaining to people his need for a normal life, and as they saw him living a regular, active life, they would treat him like other youngsters. Perhaps sometime another child, with candor and frankness, might say to him,

*"Present advances in chemotherapy have turned the picture around. In some medical centers, long-term remissions are now possible in 90 percent of children with leukemia." (*Esquire,* June 1973).

"Dan, you're going to die." If this happened, I didn't think it would be too great a jolt to Danny. He had seen lots of cowboys "die" on TV and had played the game himself many times. Also, to Danny death meant going to heaven, which would be a great adventure without any fears. So we decided that what the doctor said might be good for some, but we would share the grim fact with others. We were not to regret our decision.

We appreciated all the information the doctor gave us and were glad he gave it in a straight-forward way, using words we could understand. Before he spoke to us we had been prepared, to some extent, for what he was to say. We had received a telephone call the day before from Rena Goedhart who was a member of the Bethel Church in Bellflower where I had been pastor before coming to Canoga Park. She said, "I heard Danny has leukemia — we are very sorry." I thanked her for her concern, and we talked for a moment. Then she said, "I don't know if you have heard, but our little girl has leukemia, too." Immediately my heart went out to her as I realized their family faced the same crisis. She then told me some of the same things the doctor later told us, particularly about remission. We were grateful that she had called because it made it so much easier to hear what the doctor was to say the next day. Our minds were numb from the blow of his words, but we could rational-ly listen and understand and retain what he said. I know it is possible, under emotional distress, to hear something and yet not comprehend it at all. This was prevented by Mrs. Goedhart's thoughtfulness.

At first we found it difficult to visit with Danny. We had experienced this before when our children had polio. How do you talk to a child in the cold formality of a hospital visiting hour? A child who's usually bouncing about, absorbed in the realm of childhood fantasies, stopping only long enough to eat a cookie or ask a question or give you a hug. How do you keep from choking up inside as you see your child lying helpless there in a hospital bed?

In Danny's case, there was another complication — as there is with most children. After five minutes or so of talking with him, he would begin to ask, "When are you going home?" Not that he wanted us to. He was asking with a worried look on his face, dreading the moment when we did have to leave.

So we told him, "We have a present for you, but we're going to give it to you when we go home if you don't talk about our going home while we are here." This worked fine, and Danny didn't cry when we left.

The first Sunday following Danny's diagnosis and hospitalization was met as normally as possible. An announcement in the church bulletin stated: "Danny Brunsting is in Children's Hospital. He has leukemia. The medication now being given should restore him to active, normal health for a time. The pastor and family thank you for your love and prayers in this difficult time."

I had dreaded Sunday. I knew it would be a hard day. Preaching is an emotional strain, and I find praying to be even more emotionally taxing;

but the hardest thing of all would be to meet my beloved congregation. Why is it that when you meet someone you love for the first time following a tragedy you just sort of collapse inside? As a pastor I have often been in a home where the loved ones of the deceased are gathered and they see another loved one for the first time following the death. At this initial meeting they all begin crying. It seems so much easier to face a stranger under such circumstances than it does those we love. I think the reason is because the hearts of loved ones are open to each other. There is no barrier of reserve; the doors are open, and hearts are exposed. And I knew it would be so as I met my dear people. It was as difficult for them as it was for me to control my emotions. During the sermon I saw many weeping. But there in the pulpit I felt an aura of strength and help surrounding me. I personally believe it was an answer to the prayers of many people who were asking God's help for us. The service continued in the same way it did each Sunday morning. Our last hymn was:

> *Crown him with many crowns,*
> *The Lamb upon his throne;*
> *Hark! how the heav'nly anthem drowns*
> *All music but its own:*
> *Awake, my soul, and sing*
> *Of him who died for thee,*
> *And hail him as thy matchless King*
> *Through all eternity.*

While we sang, I felt my eyes beginning to fill — not from self-pity or sorrow, but from praise for "the Lamb" and what He meant for

Danny. Because of Him, Danny's earthly life would not end in the blackness of eternal tragedy; because of Him, Danny would be lifted on wave after wave of glory and light into Jesus' own home. Praise His Name!

On Sunday evening, John and Elaine Rex came for the evening service. At that time John was a student at Fuller Seminary, and the previous year he had served with me as a student assistant. Elaine had been the leader of our children's church. John told me that my friend Lars Granberg, then Dean of Students at Fuller and Professor of Pastoral Psychology, would ask for prayers for us at the Fuller faculty prayer meeting on Monday.

After the evening service, John and Elaine visited awhile and told us about God's care during the time, just a few years before, when their twelve-year-old daughter Sally had died of a rare type of cancer. John also showed us two verses of Scripture which he said had helped him. "Because," he said, "it gave me at least a partial answer to God's purpose in taking Sally." The verses he referred to were 2 Corinthians 1:3, 4: "Blessed be God, even the Father of our Lord Jesus Christ, the Father of mercies, and the God of all comfort; who comforteth us in all our tribulation, that we may be able to comfort them which are in any trouble, by the comfort wherewith we ourselves are comforted of God."

"Now," said John, "when I become a pastor I'll be able to bring a comfort to others which I could not have done if I had not myself experienced God's comfort when Sally died."

And I knew he could because he helped us as we talked and prayed in our living room that night. This would be one purpose God would have in our tragedy. Already He was beginning to answer our prayers that we might recognize the design He had in mind.

Other answers were to come, too. We received a letter from Emma Schmidt, our friend in Artesia. She wrote: "You are foremost in my thoughts this morning after I heard last evening of your precious little son's illness. It is, of course, a stark reminder of my own anguish of five years ago. Had our own precious Donny lived, he would have been ten years old last Tuesday. As it was, I made the doctor's appointment on his fifth birthday. Two days later we took him to the doctor, the following day to the hospital. The next day, you, as our pastor, were at the hospital with us when Dr. Spicer gave us the diagnosis. The following day, November 16, was the first of his four surgeries. Never once did I doubt that our mighty God could heal if He willed, for He who creates in secret can surely heal in secret too. Genesis 18:14 says, 'Is any thing too hard for the Lord?' And in Jeremiah 32:27 He says: 'Behold, I am the Lord, the God of all flesh: is there any thing too hard for me?' So often I'm sure we limit our God. He promises us in Ephesians 3:20 that He 'is able to do exceeding abundantly above all that we ask or think.'

"I would, of course, have preferred to keep our precious Donny here. But just think how far better for him to have been in the Lord's presence already for nearly five years now.

"At that time, you sent us a postal card and on it you wrote: 'Dear Friends, Philippians 4:19. Your pastor.' And now I would write you and say the same from one who understands. I know our God will strengthen you daily even as He has promised. Be assured of my prayers and Bethel's prayers. God bless you richly."

How well I did remember little Donny Schmidt. I remembered the text I used for his funeral. It was I Samuel 1:24: "And when she had weaned him, she took him up with her, with three bullocks, and one ephah of flour, and a bottle of wine, and brought him unto the house of the Lord in Shiloh: and the child was young." I said that Samuel had to leave his toys, playmates, home and family. This was sad. But it was only part of the picture for he was going to live in God's house in Shiloh, which would be a great adventure for a little lad. "So," I said, "Donny must now leave his toys, his playmates, and his home to go and live in God's house."

Shortly after Donny Schmidt died, someone said to me, "Donny taught Bethel to pray." I think he did, and I think this was one purpose God had for this dear little fellow. Bethel Church learned to pray in a way it had never known before.

As Samson found handfuls of honey in the carcass of a slain lion, so we would find God's sweet purposes in the midst of tragedy.

We began to think of Danny's future as a great spiritual adventure for him — the adventure of eternity. As our friends Nelson and Anne Fisher of Grand Haven, Michigan, wrote us: "Danny has such a wonderful home *here*. Mother and father, sisters and brother, and *what* a one coming!"

On Tuesday, two days before Thanksgiving, when we went to see Danny, he was getting a blood transfusion and the next day he got another. A blood transfusion looked so desperately serious. But for Danny it meant that his blood would get the cells it needed and that he would enter his remission period sooner. In that bottle was blood from some unknown donor, and as I watched it falling drop by drop through the plastic tube into Danny's arm, I wanted to thank the unknown donor, the blood bank of the Red Cross, and all who were making this help for Danny possible. I had given blood from time to time, but it was done in a rather impersonal way. Seeing those bottles by Danny's bed would make it different next time.

On Wednesday, the day before Thanksgiving, we brought Danny home. While he was receiving his blood transfusion, I made the necessary arrangements with the cashier. Then the doctor gave us the necessary instructions and the tablets that Danny was to take. Dr. Farthing had written the dosage directions on a slip of paper. That slip of paper represented the results and the application of the best of medical science. Again we were grateful to people unknown to us who had spent many hours discovering the drugs which came to us in such a small and seemingly insignificant tablet, but which would mean weeks of health and life for Danny.

Danny said good-bye to his roommates and nurses. An aide put him in a wheelchair, the elevator took us to the ground floor, and soon we were in the car and on our way home. Danny was tired but happy — and so were his daddy and mommy.

We had no idea what the months ahead would be like, but they began that afternoon with Danny and his three sisters playing with the toys he had accumulated during his week in the hospital. It was a joyful scene of happy children playing on the living room floor. One unfamiliar with the events of the previous week would never guess that lurking silent and hidden in our son's system was the Enemy — so small that it couldn't be seen, so strong that it couldn't be conquered, so tenacious that it would outlast the retaliation of science — until in the end it would accomplish its grim work.

Chapter 2

One summer afternoon in the patio garden of the American Colony in Jerusalem, the director, Bertha Spafford Vestra, told me a story of tragedy and triumph such as few people hear and almost none ever experience. After the great Chicago fire, her parents, Mr. and Mrs. H. G. Spafford, had decided to find a new life in a new land; they decided on Jerusalem. With their four children they went by train to the East Coast to board the ship which would take them to Europe. Just before sailing time Mr. Spafford was called back to Chicago on urgent business. It was decided that Mrs. Spafford and the four children would continue and Mrs. Spafford would join them later in Europe. About two-thirds of the way across the ocean their ship was struck by another and sank almost immediately. Mrs. Spafford was saved, but her four children were drowned.

Upon reaching Europe she cabled her husband, "Saved Alone."

Later as Mr. Spafford was crossing the ocean to join his wife, the ship came near the place of tragedy, and Mr. Spafford wrote these words of triumph:

> *When peace, like a river, attendeth my way,*
> *When sorrows like sea-billows roll –*
> *Whatever my lot, Thou hast taught me to say,*
> *It is well, it is well with my soul.*

Mrs. Vestra then went on to tell me how her father and mother founded the American Colony which was to give relief to suffering humanity for many generations.

"Saved Alone"! Who can understand the heartache behind those words? But here was one family who had learned that Christ opens fountains of consolation for grieving humanity which will never run dry. We were to draw water from those same fountains of consolation during Danny's predicted year of life. How else could one watch his own child day after day, knowing he would live only a year, without "going to pieces"?

In 2 Kings 20 is found the story of King Hezekiah who had a remarkable answer to prayer. "Hezekiah was sick unto death," the Bible says. Then, "Isaiah . . . came to him, and said unto him, Thus saith the Lord, Set thine house in order; for thou shalt die, and not live." When Hezekiah heard that, "he turned his face to the wall, and prayed unto the Lord, saying, I beseech thee, O Lord, remember now how I have walked before thee in truth and with a perfect heart. . . .

And Hezekiah wept sore." God was to answer that prayer, and He said, "I will add unto thy days fifteen years."

I too had "wept sore"; I too had prayed unto the Lord. But my prayer was different. When we first began to realize the seriousness of Danny's illness, even before the diagnosis had been made, I had prayed for two things. First, I asked God that if Danny could not live to please take him quickly. How much better, it seemed to me, if he had to go that it would not be by way of a long, slow process of sickness and suffering. The second request I made of God was that my wife and I might have the grace needed for whatever would be His will.

The first prayer was not to be answered as we had asked. Danny was to be taken, but not quickly. We had prayed, too, "Thy will be done" and we had meant it. Now we were beginning to see that this other way — His way — was better. Without the aid of drugs, Danny would be very sick for about three months before he would die. With the drugs he could have a normal, active life for nine months to a year and then be sick only half as long as he would have been without the drugs. This was better than what I, in my ignorance, had prayed for. Better, because I knew we would have a happy and wonderful year with our little fellow before he had to leave. Perhaps we would do more "living" during "our" year than parents usually do with their children during their entire childhood.

One of the things we naturally thought a good deal about was the home to which Danny would go when he left our home. From time to time he would say things which under other circumstances would have been ordinary, but now they had extraordinary significance. One evening after we prayed together before he went to sleep, Danny said to me, "Jesus and I are friends." I believe they were. Without special coaching from us, he showed us that he was often thinking about his "Friend" and his Friend's home.

Shortly before Christmas we were looking through a toy catalogue. He was pointing out the things he wanted for Christmas and the things he would like to get for his sisters and brother. I said, "Danny, whose birthday is it on Christmas?" He replied, "Jesus." I asked, "What do you think would be a good present for Jesus on His birthday?" He took my question seriously and looked carefully through the catalogue. I thought he found two very good presents for Jesus. His first was a world globe. He said, "I'd like to give Jesus the world." The other thing Danny found to give Jesus was a suitcase so that He could come and visit with us. I said that someday we could go and visit with Jesus. Danny thought that was fine, but wondered how we would get there. "Will we take an airplane?" he asked. "No," I answered, "God can get us there without an airplane." "Without an airplane?" He wondered how that could be, then added, "Guess He'll hold our hand." That was enough, and who can say it isn't?

One evening Danny was sitting across the table from me. He was having a little bedtime snack of toast and cereal. I looked carefully at him, as I often did during those days. He was a big boy for his age, as tall and as heavy as his sister Dorothy. On his nose, just between his eyes, was a scar. He had got that about three years before when he fell out of his high chair and struck his nose on the windowsill. I remember the morning — it was the first time I had seen a doctor sew up a cut. It was not pleasant to see the small, curved needle enter the flesh on one side of the wound and appear again on the other side. Danny also had another mark — one of his ears was a bit "flopped." We had thought some day we might like to have it straightened. He sported a butch haircut which I always gave him. His eyes were large and blue. My wife and I always enjoyed his pudgy cheeks most. They were, as Alice said, "so kissable"; and Danny always did like to be cuddled and kissed. When we would put him in bed he would always pull our heads down until our cheeks lay on his, and then he'd say, "I want to love you."

His body was strong and sturdy. He could go through a long day of play with ease. When just three years old, he learned to swim like a fish. He could go off the diving board and swim under water — he loved every minute of it. As one of our parishioners stated, "It just doesn't seem possible that that bouncing boy could possibly be fatally ill."

Danny had a pleasant disposition. I think it might be characterized by saying that he loved life. He always entered everything in high spirits and with a happy-go-lucky attitude. He loved to play, to laugh and giggle, to run and jump. We always thought of him as a great little guy.

I thought as I sat looking at him that day: *Dear little Danny, how can it be you're so sick that it can end in nothing but death? Little Danny boy, why must this be?* I know he, too, was puzzled. One day as he sat on the floor, I saw him hike up his pant legs and stare for a long time at his legs; then he rubbed them with his hands. Finally I overheard him say, "What's wrong with my legs anyway?"

Danny, Danny, what a strange thing this is! Here you are so alive, so real, so much ours, and yet you are these things so temporarily.

About this time someone volunteered this thought, "It certainly is fortunate that you do have four other children." I would certainly have to agree. But this cannot mean that the passing of a child is of less significance when one has five children than, say, if there were only one. Suppose the total love of parents for their children is stated as 100 percent. If they have five children, it does not mean that each child has 20 percent of their love. No, love is not cut and divided like a pie. Each child, whether there be one or ten, gets 100 percent of the love. And it seems logical that the more we have to love, the more love we have for each.

This fact from life helps me understand God better. "God is love." It helps me understand something of the Trinity. Each person of the Holy Trinity is not one-third of God, any more than three children would each receive one-third of their parents' love. So Jesus is all God, the Father is all God, the Holy Spirit is all God. This can be because God is love, and each of the persons of the Trinity is 100 percent God, 100 percent love; and the three are One, and the One is love. It helps me understand, too, the relation of us children to our heavenly Father. God is love, God loves us, and all of His love is for each of us! Because this is true, we can believe what William Cowper wrote in 1774:

> God moves in a mysterious way
> His wonders to perform;
> He plants his footsteps in the sea,
> And rides upon the storm.
>
> Deep in unfathomable mines
> Of never-failing skill
> He treasures up his bright designs,
> And works his sovereign will.
>
> Ye fearful saints, fresh courage take;
> The clouds ye so much dread
> Are big with mercy, and shall break
> In blessings on your head.
>
> ·················
> Blind unbelief is sure to err,
> And scan his work in vain;
> God is his own interpreter,
> And he will make it plain.

Love is to be the relationship among the members of the human race. And increasing the number of people loved never decreases the amount of love for each but, amazingly enough, actually increases it. And in God we see the ultimate of this strange formula. God has such an unfathomable capacity for love because He loves everyone! We must agree with Henry Drummond's summary of 1 Corinthians 13, love is "the greatest thing in the world."

Mahalia Jackson, known as one of the world's greatest gospel singers, said that her people cry when a child is born and rejoice when he goes to be with the Lord. This is so unnatural and so uncommon as to give rise to considerable thought. But I could understand it if two conditions were present: if the world into which the child was born was one of great difficulty and hardship, and also if there was firm faith that the world into which the child would go by death would be one of ultimate bliss and peace. For the race which produced the great Negro spirituals, both of these conditions were present. As I watched my son, a big black cowboy hat on his head, a wad of gum in his mouth, his face animated by the play-life of a boy, I thought, *how will it be possible to rejoice when he goes to be with the Lord?*

God gave a remarkable peace concerning this matter for which we were profoundly grateful. My wife wrote in a letter: "When I hold Danny on my lap and sing or read to him, it seems the whole thing is impossible. Yet God has given us peace of mind and heart about it." Some years ago I had heard a radio sermon by my friend Bob Schuler on the text, "I have learned, in whatsoever state I am, therewith to be content" (Phil. 4:11). A few verses later Paul tells the source of this amazing ability. "I can do all things through Christ which strengtheneth me" (Phil. 4:13). Bob had illustrated his sermon from various areas of life. Could we be content — satisfied with our state? "Through Christ" it would be possible!

Danny was receiving considerable attention and getting many presents. This was not easy for his sister Dorothy. One morning she told us, "I can't walk." Then she proceeded to limp, as Danny had done when we first noticed his ailment. When she was sitting on the floor, she would get up by placing the palms of her hands first on the floor then on her knees, laboriously getting up into a standing position. This was all part of a kind of reverse empathy. We knew she was putting on a clever act, and it rather amused us. It also taught us several important lessons. It showed us that even though Danny was sick and needed special care and help, we did need to be careful. It would be easy for him to become spoiled. If this were to happen, he couldn't be happy nor could the family. Alice and I decided that discipline would be employed as needed. Dorothy's little act also reminded us that we had four other children who would continue to need our affection and attention. We were careful to see that they got it.

On December 4 I received an invitation from a church in Denver to preach each day during Holy Week. Under normal circumstances, this invitation from Denver would probably have been accepted. Now it could not be. I was thinking of James 4:13, 14: "Go to now, ye that say, Today or tomorrow we will go into such a city, and continue there a year, and buy and sell, and get gain: Whereas ye know not what shall be on the morrow." I wrote them the following letter:

My Dear Friends,

Your letter inviting me to speak during Holy Week recalls many pleasant hours and happy associations I have had in Denver. I do wish I could accept your invitation, but I find it impossible to do so.

I can make only very limited and tentative plans regarding the future because of an illness which has come into our family. Our youngest child Danny, age four, has been stricken with leukemia. We never know what may happen from one day to the next. With the use of modern medicine we may anticipate that he will have nine months to a year of normal active life, but it is uncertain. Under such circumstances it would be unwise for me to make any definite plans.

We would appreciate the prayers of our friends in Denver. I will pray that you will have God's guidance in making other arrangements for Holy Week and for the services.

This letter indicates a realization of the uncertainty of life we had never known so clearly before. It is not that we couldn't know it. The Bible speaks frequently about it and I had often expressed the idea in funeral messages. But how often we take such so theoretically. For us there would now be much more meaning in the words, "Ye know not what shall be on the morrow."

This uncertainty of life has a great lesson to teach us that we saw again and again in connection with Danny. We and all who knew him were painfully mindful of his prognosis. This tempered our relationship with him with all possible sweetness, care, concern, love, and prayers. This seemed so right and natural that any other conduct with a dying child is inconceivable. Isn't this essentially, however, the situation of every person we meet? In Danny's case it was exaggerated because we knew so definitely, but the truest thing we can say about anybody is that he is dying. We belong to a race of dying people — this is universally true. Should not every association, then, be mellowed with the kindness and tenderness and affection we show for the one whose dying has become more real because of a medical prediction?

Because we knew what was going to happen, little neglected deeds of love and affection were done. For example Danny's bike, a hand-me-down from Bernie to Carol to Dorothy, was long in need of repair. Now it was done. I bought a new tire and painted the bike a bright red and white as Danny watched with sparkling eyes. A little bell was put on the handle bars. He was delighted with it. As I worked, I wondered how often little deeds of kindness are left undone and how often the more important aspects of our relationships with our fellow-man are also neglected simply because we are not mindful of the uncertainty of life.

The uncertainty of life not only points up the matter of doing for others, but it also creates a fuller quality of appreciation. Knowing Danny had just a year or so of life certainly made us appreciate him in a way which would never have been realized under ordinary circumstances. During those days, I often thought of two fathers in the Bible. The one was Abraham, who took the road to Mt. Moriah with his son, thinking he would return alone. The Bible does not tell us what his thoughts were, but of one thing I am sure: He had a fuller sense of appreciation for his son than he had ever had before. Another father I often think of is David who had a son who was ill, and it was such a grievous thing to this father that he could not eat. For all people this uncertainty of life is true; and since it is true, shouldn't there be a greater awareness of the needs of others, of the help we can give them, and a greater appreciation for them?

Because we knew that Danny would not grow up, we had a "privilege" parents don't often have — we could let Danny be a boy. Just purely and simply a boy without loading him with the burden of becoming a man. It is surprising how much of parents' attention is directed toward making their children "grow up." Now we weren't in the least concerned about conforming Danny into some manly pattern. We let him be 100 percent boy, and he flourished in that kind of atmosphere. After all, what is so superior about being grown up? Is adulthood so much better that we need to force its behavior patterns on our children? In the realm of the Spirit, at least, Jesus gave us to understand that in the child there is something that adults need to emulate. His word was "Whosoever shall not receive the kingdom of God as a little child, he shall not enter therein" (Mark 10:15). And what is so true of the kingdom of God is true of human life in many ways. A child, when allowed to really be a child, has such honest-to-goodness fun that adults can be envious. Instead of walking, children bounce and skip. My wife has often remarked that some of the most delightful sounds in the world are the little squeals of sheer delight from the children; yet how peaceful and calm the sleep of a tired child is. We had no reason to force adult behavior patterns on Danny. He was a child, all child, and we greatly enjoyed it.

After Danny had been home a few weeks, he started to feel much better, and locomotion slowly returned to his legs. The neurologist told us that we could expect him to have full use of his legs. However, as Danny continued to make improvement, it became increasingly difficult to be reconciled to his death. When a person is pale, sickly, and obviously in grave physical weakness, death seems not only a real possibility but also the normal and inevitable outcome. As a pastor I had frequently viewed it in such a light as I stood and watched and heard the last labored breathing of a dying person. But when there is life and health and strength, death seems remote and unreal.

We received the assurances of the concern, love, and prayers of people all across America. Our lives had come in contact with people in many parts of the country. They knew, they cared, they shared. This was a constant source of strength. Others, however, did not know. There would be things said that would hurt. One such instance happened in the drugstore where I went to have Danny's prescription filled. The drug was, of course, seldom dispensed. In fact, this was the first time it had been dispensed by this particular pharmacy. The pharmacist said to me, "My partner told me there is no sense in ordering that drug. He bet me it would never move." Then with a big grin of elation he added, "Guess I won my bet, didn't I?" What may be to one a matter of indifference or even amusement may often be to another a matter of deep concern and grief. How very careful, how tender, how loving must be our relations with others. This big family of human beings is so much in need of our care, our compassion, and our help.

When Danny first became sick, we asked the Lord to let this experience express His love and grace. We knew it could serve Him, for God had used this bitter experience of polio in our family for His glory. We received a helpful letter concerning this from a boyhood friend, Harold Colenbrander. He wrote:

Dear Friends:

We have been carrying you on our hearts and in our prayers, since we learned last week that one of your little ones has leukemia. The *Holland City News* carried the report, and we have been burdened for you.

It has often been said that God fits the burden to the back, and I am sure God has great confidence in you in bringing to you this trial of your faith. It has appeared to me that God has been honored by your victories of faith, and I can only believe He shall be glorified by you again.

We have not ceased to wonder why so much of God's goodness should come to our lives and home, while others have so much more trial and sadness. While we are very grateful for all God has done for us, we would indeed be selfish if we did not try to share our brother's burden. We want to assure you of our concern and of our prayers which we shall offer up regularly in your behalf.

Some friends of ours in Holland had a little boy with the same illness, and we were blessed by them as the victories of their faith were shared with us. It is still true that in all things God is working for our good. We trust that someday we'll be able to understand the wonders of His way.

It is our prayer that in the Christ of Bethlehem you may see again God's love for you and your family, and that because of His love and grace you may enjoy a very blessed Christmas season.

Sincerely,
Harold and Frances

This letter was a real blessing to us. It gave us a clue to God's meaning and purpose. The sentence that was particularly helpful and valuable was: "It has appeared to me that God has been honored by your victories of faith, and I can only believe He shall be glorified by you again." For this, I was praying. And this prayer would be answered, it seemed to me, if two things came to be. First, if I testified of the peace God was giving in answer to prayer, and second, if this burden could be used to help others.

Alice and I were both amazed and grateful that we could testify to the serenity and peace God was giving. After our regular prayer meeting one evening, a lady said to me that she was very disappointed that no one had prayed specifically for us. She said, "I am sure you were deeply upset and distressed because of this omission." Nothing could have been further from the truth. It was difficult for the people to audibly express their feelings in prayer concerning this matter. But I knew that with their tender and loving hearts they were bringing our needs to God. I felt the strength and help of those silent hearts. I was not "upset and distressed." In fact, there was such a

strength, such a peace that it truly "passed understanding," and for which I had only one explanation — God was answering prayer. God would be
glorified as others came to know that for us, "God
is a very present help in trouble."

The second way in which this experience could
honor God would be if others could be helped by
it. It has frequently been said that we are saved
to serve; it can also be said that we suffer to serve,
and there is a unique service that comes from
suffering. There was much spiritual help and
service that we could now bring to humanity that
would never otherwise have been possible. This
was true because we now held a more sensitive
and understanding attitude towards the needs of
others, and we had learned what is helpful to
others in time of need.

We certainly did not want to capitalize on our
experience, but we did want to use it for the glory
of God and the help of humanity. At this time I
was preaching from the Book of Acts. We were
up to the fourth chapter, and I used the twenty-
ninth verse for my text: "And now, Lord, behold
their threatenings: and grant unto thy servants,
that with all boldness they may speak thy word."
My sermon subject was "When Life Grows Difficult." I made no direct reference to our
particular circumstance, but a certain power and
persuasiveness penetrated the message that was
born from personal experience. That message
reflected our attitude to the tragedy that had
come into our life. I said, "We go along so little
touched by the tragedies of life, and then suddenly the impossible happens to us." I asked the

congregation, "Then what do we do? It is our reaction to the storm, rather than the storm itself, which determines whether it will be triumph or tragedy." I suggested several inadequate refuges man seeks from the storms of life, such as self-pity, rebellion, and drink; but for the Christian there is God. And as the disciples found Him through prayer in the midst of "their threatenings," so, too, can we find Him.

Next, I tried to show the disciples' concept of God. He was the Creator. To Him they said, "Lord, thou art God, which hast made heaven, and earth, and the sea, and all that in them is" (verse 24). "We need," I said, "a conviction concerning the Almightiness of God." However, power without wisdom and love is despotism. The God with whom they found refuge was the God of wisdom and love. To this God they prayed and said, "and grant. . . ." Grant what? That *their* circumstances might be altered? Grant that they might escape? No, they prayed that in all circumstances, pleasant or otherwise, they might be loyal and true to God and that they might have the strength and serenity to triumph. When Jesus faced the cross, He was human enough to want to escape "the cup," but there was something He wanted even more — that was to do the will of God. I also spoke of the result of the disciples' prayer. The passage tells us that God, the Holy Spirit, came into their lives in such a real and thrilling way that they were true and faithful, and from their "threatenings" came a glorious triumph. "They spake the word of God with boldness" — so much so that we speak of them as having "great grace."

I closed the sermon with two quotations from the Bible: "Cast all your anxieties on him, for he cares about you" (1 Pet. 5:7, RSV); or as translated by J. B. Phillips: "You can throw the whole weight of your anxieties upon him, for you are his personal concern." The other quotation was from Philippians 4:6, 7: "Have no anxiety about anything, but in everything by prayer and supplication with thanksgiving let your requests be made known to God. And the peace of God, which passes all understanding, will keep your hearts and your minds in Christ Jesus" (RSV); or again as translated by Phillips: "Don't worry over anything whatever; tell God every detail of your needs in earnest and thankful prayer, and the peace of God, which transcends human understanding, will keep constant guard over your hearts and minds as they rest in Christ Jesus."

In psychology books I have seen lists and explanations of escape mechanisms which we use to avoid unpleasant situations in life. To the list found in psychology books I would now add another: "faith healing."

One day a lady who attended our church came to see me, her face animated with an urgency as though she had a message of God for me. She stated that she had detected unbelief in my heart concerning God's healing power. She added that such unbelief would, in all probability, prevent the cure and healing God could give. She then quoted for me the verse, "He could do no mighty works there because of their unbelief." I believe these things were said to me out of a sincere desire to help and because of real love and concern, but what she said was really demoralizing. It was an attempted escape from reality under the subterfuge of a superior brand of spirituality.

I wonder how many people have been subjected to this misguided torture? I wonder how many sick have come with faith and hope to a "faith healer" and have gone home with an added burden of guilt when told, "You don't have sufficient faith"? What is so often missed is that it is not a matter of faith in healing, but of faith in God and acceptance of His will.

In regard to our son, it seemed to me there were three possibilities available to God. One, Danny could be healed by a direct act of God; two, Danny could be healed through a new discovery in medicine; or three, the disease could run its usual course. We believed all three of these were real possibilities, but we did not feel that we should make the choice and then through prayer attempt to coerce God to make it come true. We did pray for Danny's recovery. We did pray with the understanding that God would make the choice. And we did pray for the faith necessary to face the reality of His choice.

The escape mechanism of "faith healing" is similar in some ways to the attitude expressed by unbelievers. Some who spoke to us would say something like this, "Oh, it just can't be!" Here was the same unwillingness to face the unpleasant realities of life. On the part of most of our friends these two forms of escape were avoided as they faced this tragic reality with us and asked God to give us the strength to face it and the understanding to use it for His glory.

One day Alice said to me, "Have you ever thought of how God must have felt when the plans were being made for the sacrifice of His Son for sin?" I think we both came to understand much more clearly how He did feel. It is an overwhelming, unfathomable, indescribable love which will give up a Son for an undeserving people. Many parents never have the experience of knowing in advance that they are going to lose their child. Few see their children alive and active, as we were experiencing, and yet know the end is near. But this was the kind of experience God had, since before the foundations of the earth it had been decided that His Son would execute the plan of Redemption. This was known and certainly felt by God. Perhaps we experienced just a small part of that experience of God as day after day we lived and played with our dear son, knowing he must become sick and die. The love God had for mankind to go through that kind of experience became more evident to us.

I was thinking about these things one day as I sat by Danny's bed in the hospital while he was getting a blood transfusion. He was awfully good about this rather painful ordeal. Once the needle had pierced the flesh of his little arm, he didn't seem to mind too much. But that needle plunged just as surely into my heart as it did into his arm. What a false and blasphemous picture of God it is to think that He was calmly getting His satisfaction through the cruel tortures of His Son on the Cross. When it tells us in Isaiah 53:5 that "he was wounded for our transgressions, he was bruised for our iniquities," it is speaking of God the Father just as surely as it is speaking of God the Son. The vicarious suffering of parents for their child is as real as the suffering of the child. Oh, how readily I would have taken Danny's sufferings so that he might know relief — because I loved him. God, because He loved us, planned and carried out that salvation by which He could take our sufferings so that the "chastisement of our peace was upon Him." I could agree with my wife that we were being taken a little deeper into the things of God. This was sacred and holy ground, and every step of the way filled us with awe and reverence.

A few weeks after Danny's illness was diagnosed as leukemia, we arranged for him to be under the care of Dr. Brubaker of the Hematology Department of Children's Hospital. We were grateful for his careful explanation of Danny's condition in terms we could understand. He told us that ten years before nothing could have been done for leukemia except blood transfusions. Now, he explained, the new drugs were able to throw a chemical block in the road of the disease so that temporarily it would be thwarted. However, the disease was "smart" and within a few months would learn a way around the block. When that happened a new drug would be used. When the disease began to overcome the drug, it could be predicted by the taking and testing of the bone marrow. This bone marrow test would be taken by giving a local anesthetic at the hip and plunging a large needle through the skin, tissues, and bone into the marrow. It would be painful but lasted only a few minutes. This would be done every month or so. As the effectiveness of the drug began to subside, it would be detected, and before Danny would be sick again he would be switched to a new drug.

I asked the doctor, "Do you think a cure for this disease is coming?" He answered, "Yes, I do think it is coming. If I didn't, I couldn't continue to work in this field." Then I asked him, "Could it come at any moment?" He said, "I know of nothing now that will produce it. However, when it does come, it will probably come overnight. Fifty to sixty thousand drugs have been tested; each testing may represent research for as many as five years. So far, only three groups of drugs are effective. When a cure does come," he went on, "it will probably be in the nature of a control such as insulin is for the diabetic." He told us he would keep us constantly apprised of any new developments in the field.

The morning the doctor told us this, Danny had a blood-marrow test. It indicated that the marrow was still predominantly leukemic but that the very first change in the battle to arrest the disease had begun. We were thankful for this, as in some few cases this doesn't happen. When I carried Danny back to the car, my eyes swam with tears as I thought, *only God will ever know how much I love this boy.*

"Daddy," Danny said to me, "the nurse told me I was a good boy." *You are, Danny. You are!* I thought.

On the afternoon of Sunday, December 14, I received a call from a member of the church to tune in to the TV program "Conquest" on

Channel 2. The program was giving a report on leukemia research. We saw how thousands of scientists all over the world were engaged in research to find an answer to this dread disease. There were two things in the program that particularly impressed me. At one point a doctor said, "A few years ago we could do nothing for a child with leukemia — then we were able to give them a few months. Now it is possible to give them a year or more of useful life." The thing that struck me was the word "useful." I had never thought before of a child being "useful." Yet in so many ways this is just what Danny had become to us and others. We had learned much about the ways of God, the uncertainty of life, the need for compassion and understanding for humanity, and many other valuable lessons. He was a constant message from God to us. One might say he was "useful." I would say "very useful."

The other impression made by the program was that a cure or control was imminent; it could occur at any time. Someone had asked me how I felt they should pray for Danny. I wasn't sure at the time. I was in agreement with my dear friend Reverend Bert VanSoest who said, "We always pray for God's healing power of mercy until we are sure He wills otherwise, and then we pray for God's grace to submit." I had also prayed in a rather vague way, I'm afraid, that the cure or control for leukemia might be found. After the TV program, it became clear to me how I should pray. I should pray specifically that medical science would find the answer. The next morning I began the first of what became a daily time of prayer for this particular purpose. That Monday morning on my knees before God I felt entirely in the Lord's will in making this request of the Lord.

"O God," I prayed, "You have laid it on my heart to pray for the men of science that by Thy grace they may somewhere, somehow find what is needed to control or to cure leukemia." I prayed morning after morning in a special time of prayer devoted to this request. I was encouraged in many ways to continue and the first encouragement came on that first day that I began to pray in this way. We had to take Danny to Children's Hospital for another transfusion. While there, I talked with two doctors about the program I had watched on TV, and both heartily agreed that the search could end in success at any moment. This, to me, was a green light to continue my prayers. A second encouragement came that same day. After Danny's transfusion, he was the best we had ever seen him. Certainly this had nothing at all to do with the finding of a cure, and yet to me it was a message of encouragement. When Danny got home that day, he was walking much better than he had before. He was proud and happy with his accomplishment. Then with a radiance on his face and in his eyes that we hadn't seen since he became sick, he looked at me and said, "I'm not going to get sick again!" Would my prayers and the similar prayers of many others be answered? Would Danny's prediction come to pass? That night our family dinner table was the merriest and gayest it had been for weeks.

A third encouragement came the very next morning. On Tuesday, December 16, our morning paper, *The Los Angeles Times,* carried a news article which told how the government had spent $30,000,000 so far that year investigating cancer in an effort to develop a drug which would cure the disease.

This was not only a further encouragement to me to continue my daily period of prayer for this matter, but it also gave me a great idea. Here were thousands of dedicated scientists spending their time and talent in research and the government had spent $30,000,000 on this project in less than one year. Now, it seemed to me, that this great team of science and government should have as an ally people who would pray for this same project. If our scientists were willing to spend the time and talent and our government the money necessary to find a cure or control for cancer, surely God's people would be willing to join with them, giving their efforts in the way in which they were qualified — through prayer. I could ask the people of our church to join with me in such a daily prayer effort, and I knew of others who would. Perhaps we could gather a great team of interested people who would form a praying partnership to be allied with the medical profession and the government in challenging the disease of cancer.

I did not have in mind only the saving of my son. Certainly I would pray that it would come in time for him, but if it didn't, I could encourage my prayer partners to continue praying with me until the answer came. So I asked God to give me direction in finding those who would join with me in daily prayer that the cure and control of cancer might be found.

Chapter 3

How does a boy, almost four, spend his days? I had never thought of that before. Sometimes, to be sure, I had played with our children or watched them play. I had observed them at meals and other times, but I certainly was in no position to make a report on how a four-year-old spends his time. Now I began to observe, and it was fascinating. Children live in a world of much delight. They notice, touch, taste, see, and do things which bring them into contact with so much that escapes our adult attention.

About a week before Christmas the seven of us filled our station wagon for a ride through a section of Tarzana where homeowners had decorated their lawns, trees, and homes with lighted Christmas themes. One street was "Candy Cane Lane," another "Santa Claus Lane," another "Carol Lane," etc. With a delightful display of ingenuity expressed in color and lights, these people provided our family with a pleasant hour of entertainment. Danny was particularly impressed with the hundreds and hundreds of colored lights. Lights seem so appropriate and right at Christmas time when we remember the "Light of the World" who came that men need no longer walk in darkness.

After dinner that night, we trimmed our Christmas tree. We had a big one, so big the star touched the ceiling. Danny said, "Hey, look, our star is in the sky!" As always, the children had great fun putting the "rain" and colored balls on the tree. While they were finishing it, Danny and I sat in a big chair together. Each tiny, colored bulb was reflected in Danny's eyes as he stared in fascination at the magic which had come into our living room. After the trimming of the tree, Danny watched *Rin-Tin-Tin,* his favorite TV program, and then it was bedtime.

Danny liked the big room he slept in, and it was good to see him there. The room had seemed so empty while he was in the hospital. But it was not empty at all when Danny was there. The floor was covered with a candy-stripe carpet, and on the walls were pictures cut from wood. One was a horse with the rider several inches above in the process of being bucked off, but he was still holding to the rope with which he had lassoed a calf. Danny enjoyed this and other pictures he had on his wall. On his desk there were two plastic horses, each with a rider. One was the Lone Ranger, and the other was the bad guy he called the "Lone Stranger." Many an hour these two cowboys had been gripped in fierce play-battle with each other. When Danny went to bed, he liked to have someone with him for a while, someone who would read a story, pray, and talk.

With all our children we have found that this is a most precious time. It is a time when they share the experiences and thoughts of their young lives. It is then that a parent can be closer to his child than at any other time. Danny especially liked the "smootchings" which closed the good-night rituals before he fell asleep on his side with both hands under his cheek, sort of like a cherub.

Another time of close fellowship which Danny shared with the family was evening dinner. Every dinner was "special." To create the right atmosphere we always ate in the dining room which had a fireplace. Danny loved to stretch out before the fire on the floor. Then as the flames began to dance and leap, his eyes would do the same. The lights were dimmed and the candles were lit on the table, and their soft, mellow glow gave us a nice atmosphere for the hour. Here the interests of school, the newspaper, and life were shared and commented on. Even if our fare was the hot dog or the hamburger, as it often was, we had all the charm and none of the cost of a high-class restaurant. The meal concluded with our evening prayers. Each child had a Bible and read a verse in turn from the chapter of the night. Dorothy and Danny, too young to read, each got a lap to sit on. Occasionally there would be a comment or question, then prayer. Each got his turn. Danny's prayer always began, "Jesus died on the cross for our sin," and he never failed to remember the missionaries.

Our family loved games. There was usually a game of Scrabble, checkers, chess, or Monopoly going on. These often began before breakfast in the morning. Danny was too young for these games, but he loved to play most anything. One of his favorite games was wrestling. When he would say to me, "Let's play, daddy," it usually meant wrestling. He would grunt and groan in true style as he would force me to the ground. He meant to be "tough," but he couldn't help but giggle when I got him down because I would pivot my head in his tummy until he shook with laughter.

As parents, we soon learned that the cost of a toy does not determine its play value. During those days, Danny's favorite toy was the scraps of lumber left by the carpenters who were building our new church. These odd-sized bits of wood turned into churches, bridges, or railroad tracks as he laid them end to end. The song which says "The Best Things in Life Are Free" is true. For a child it may be a discarded cardboard box or some scrap lumber; for me a flaming sunset as the shadows begin to drop like a shawl over the shoulders of the hills in our lovely valley or the warm and cheerful smile of a friend are some of the "best things in life."

Another favorite game of Danny's, which cost nothing, was to crawl in bed with dad and mother. This was done the first thing in the morning. There under the warm covers we would talk and laugh together. At other times Danny and I sat together in a big chair to read a story or look at pictures. In our big chair we took excursions into all parts of the world via the pictures of the *National Geographic* magazine. We went on many an adventure together, sometimes "shivering" in the cold Arctic, sometimes "sweating" under a hot Africa sun, but always having fun.

Christmas week! The most exciting week of the year for a child! Gaily colored packages of potential delight began appearing under the tree. How does a four-year-old keep from discovering their mysteries? Danny managed only with great difficulty. On Sunday afternoon the annual Sunday School Christmas Program was held. Danny sat on my lap during most of the program. He didn't participate with his class; he hadn't been with them for practice, and his walk was still too stiff and difficult to negotiate a trip to the stage. *Would this be Danny's last Christmas?* I asked myself. *What about next year?*

We let the happiness of that hour shove such thoughts from our minds. William Saroyan wrote in his Christmas poem, "Christmas is being together." No family could be more conscious of "being together" that Christmas than we were.

The day before Christmas I wrapped a stack of New Testaments, beautifully bound in blue, which I was going to give to all the men who were working on the new church building. Danny watched and questioned the procedure. The next morning when he had crawled into bed with us, he explained to his mother about the "little Bibles," "Daddy's going to give them to all the carpenters. Some of them are Christians and some of them aren't. Mommy, what is a Christian?"

"What do you think a Christian is, Danny?" mother asked.

"Somebody that goes to church," Danny answered. "And," he added after he thought a moment, "somebody who loves Jesus." Mommy and Danny both agreed it was a good idea to give our workers a New Testament. There in bed, the day before Christmas, a little boy not yet four prayed with his mother for those who would get a New Testament that day. Next day, with shuffling gait, Danny helped me distribute them to the workers.

The carpenters had come to know and like Danny and Dorothy. Before Danny became sick, he and Dorothy would have their noon lunch put up in a sack and then go out and eat with the workers. This was real "big," and they and the workers enjoyed it. One of the carpenters brought Danny a present several days before Christmas. The carpenter told Danny to "go ahead and open it." He rightly figured that if he had one to open before Christmas, the difficulty of waiting would be relieved. It was a big, long, red fire engine that knew how to shoot out a stream of water! Marge VanLente, a friend of the family, brought him a bright red plastic fireman's helmet to go with it. Danny had often watched the big engines with their brave men roaring past our place to brush fires in the hills around our valley. Now Danny, with the vivid imagination of a boy, became a fireman. What a right combination — a spirited boy, a fireman's helmet, and a fire truck really squirting water. All we needed was a fire, and we arranged that too!

Our dining room fireplace became the scene of many a pitched battle between a gallant fireman and a roaring fire.

Danny received many toys for Christmas, of which one was a doctor case that he had requested. He enjoyed being the family "Doc." He would persuade one of us to be sick, and his examination was very thorough. The use of the stethoscope and other instruments was familiar to him. He took blood tests and gave shots with an unnatural familiarity for a boy not yet four. His voice was grave and professional as he would intone, "You are very sick, but we can make you better," or, "This is going to hurt, but only for a minute — now be brave." His "pills" were usually administered with this advice, "When I was a little boy, I took a pill every day and it made me well; you better take yours too."

Except for a slight stiffness in his walk, Danny was back to normal by the Sunday after Christmas. But the realization of his true condition never left us. We were shown what faced us in a letter we received from Floyd and Dorothy Menning. Floyd, a minister in the hills of Kentucky, had received and accepted a call to start a new church just a few miles from us. Just a few days after Christmas he wrote:

Dear Friends:

The Lord has called our baby Paul to His heavenly home. He had been in Louisville Children's Hospital one week with a minor infection when suddenly his heart collapsed and he went quickly and quietly in his sleep.

Truly we have found God's grace sufficient through this trial. His comfort and peace are wonderful.

Their child had had a congenital heart condition from birth. While he lived, they had constantly faced the bleak prospect of possible death. I wondered how we would face that hour. I wrote them: "To one who has given himself and his all to God, no word of comfort is needed; to one who has not, no word of comfort is sufficient."

What these parents now faced, we were facing by anticipation. I could not refrain from thinking, thinking, thinking about how it all must end. What would the final sickness be like? And having conducted so many funerals, I could not help but think what that would be like. An overwhelming sorrow filled my soul as I thought of active, spirited, bouncing Danny being still and cold in death. Sometimes as I went about my work, this thought would bring a flash flood of tears to my eyes. Sometimes during the church service a line of a hymn would carry me away in imagination to that future hour when there would be some similar music at the funeral of a dear little boy. There is no manual of instruction on how to face such a situation, but there are aids.

One was expressed in a letter from my friend Dr. John R. Mulder, then President of Western Seminary. He wrote, "The best counsel I can offer is to school yourselves to live within each day, and to accept the package of grace that comes for that day." If I could only drop a sluice gate between the present and the irretrievable yesterday and another between the present and the unpredictable tomorrow. "Sufficient unto the day is the evil thereof," Jesus taught. Yet we insist on borrowing the probable heartaches and tears of tomorrow and add them to today. I tried to school myself to live within each day.

Another aid, I found, was to divert my attention to some other object. Bishop Francis Paget wrote in *The Spirit of Discipline:*

> *There is another very safe and simple way to escape when the dull mood begins to gather round one, and that is to turn as promptly and as strenuously as one can to whatever work one can at the moment do. It was excellent advice of Mr. Keble's, "When you find yourself overpowered as it were by melancholy, the best way is to go out, and do something kind to somebody or other."*

How often a walk with the children or an hour's play with them kept me from slipping into the "slough of Despond."

On the Monday morning after Christmas we were made happy by what the doctor told us. In the first place Danny had definitely entered remission. This was determined from his blood test. His blood had not lost ground since his transfusion a week before. We had already guessed this by his general condition which appeared better to us on Sunday than any time since his return from the hospital. The doctor also told us that in his opinion Danny's life expectancy might easily be one and a half to two years. Until then we had been thinking in terms of nine months to a year. These extra months looked very good to us. Danny did not need a blood transfusion, and the doctor told us we would not have to return until January 15. Danny was delighted to escape a bone marrow test and transfusion, and we were happy about the good news we had heard. On the way home my wife said, "I feel better now than I have at any time since Danny became ill." We celebrated by using a bit of Danny's Christmas money to buy him the derrick crane he wanted to go with his new dump truck.

Shortly after the new year began, I attended a ministers' retreat at Alpine Conference Grounds near Lake Arrowhead. I have always greatly enjoyed and been much impressed by the scenic wonder of the mountains. Somehow God seems closer among the towering pines of the forests. Perhaps it is because in the mountains I have seen hundreds of young people give their lives to Jesus Christ in summer youth camps.

There were about twenty of my fellow ministers present at the retreat. We all felt a closer fellowship and a more definite working of God's Spirit than we had experienced before in our annual retreats. The first afternoon we spent time discussing the matter of physical healing in answer to prayer. On our knees we prayed before God. Some felt led to pray that God would heal Danny. Others prayed that a cure or control for cancer might be found. I was deeply appreciative of the love and concern of my fellow ministers. It was such a helpful experience that even now as I think of it my heart fills with emotion. I was asked to lead the closing service held before we returned to our homes. I read Genesis 22, which records the story of Abraham and Issac.

I told the men that a number of years ago I had heard Dr. Larry Love speak at the Gull Lake Bible Conference in Michigan. I shared with my fellow ministers one statement which Larry made to us at the time — a statement I had often thought about. He said he had come to the point in his life where he was able to say to God that he was willing to lose his family — his own children and wife — if necessary for the sake of obeying God. This impressed me as an illustration of amazing obedience. It was an Abraham kind of obedience. Abraham could, as far as he knew, obey God and lose his son or disobey God and keep his son. As it turned out he obeyed God *and* kept his son, but this he did not know when he made his decision to obey.

I said to the men that obedience was the bridge of connection between what God has said and what we do. "If the choice were now mine to choose between obeying God and losing my son or disobeying God and keeping my son, I couldn't honestly say what I would choose. The quick answer might be, 'We'll obey God regardless of the consequences.' But this is only the quick answer; more reflection will remind us that we frequently disobey for a much less significant reason than the keeping of a child." Of course, God was not giving me the choice; I only wondered what I would do if I did have the choice. Larry Love, by God's grace, could say, "I will choose obedience, even if it means the loss of my family." This retreat, one of the richest spiritual experiences of my life, closed with testimonies as to the blessings of the hours we had spent together and the decisions we had made. We then each found a place where we could be alone on our knees before God. Hearts were melted and tears flowed as we met our God in prayer. This was a spiritual blessing of the first magnitude.

When I got home and drove the car into our yard, Danny was playing on the driveway. He was riding his trike, his black cowboy hat pulled down low over his eyes. With one hand he was steering, while the other was pulling the wagon. He was lost in a dream world of play. Perhaps in his imagination he was astride the plunging lead horse of a great team pulling a stage through the sage of a western desert. Maybe it was a runaway, and he was engaged in a daring episode of rescue. I thought, *"Danny, my dear son, keep riding! riding! riding!"*

About a year before Danny became sick, a man of our church who was a representative of Forest Lawn Cemetery asked for an appointment. His purpose was to sell our family burial lots. I told him that being a minister and therefore subject to change of residence I did not think we should purchase any lots. I was also thinking that surely we would not be needing any cemetery lots for a long time to come. *Does one buy cemetery lots when he is only thirty-five?* I asked myself. The salesman did make a point, however, which seemed reasonable and right to me, and that was that such preparations as he was suggesting could best be made before they were actually needed. At the time of need there is an emotional and mental strain which may not be conducive to sound judgment.

It seemed to me wise counsel for the things of the spirit, too. The Bible instructs in Ecclesiastes 12:1 that we make our preparation "before the evil days come." I suppose some spiritual moorings are found in the crisis of tragedy and affliction — "there are no atheists in foxholes" — but sound, sure, and thorough spiritual foundations should be laid in more untroubled days.

An experience from the life of Dwight L. Moody is an illustration of such preparation. While he was crossing the Atlantic, the ship was attacked by a violent storm. Some of the passengers went to pray together. When they asked Mr. Moody to join them, he replied, "I'm all prayed up." I think a man can be "all prayed up" and still do some praying when the storm comes. But an emergency is a little late for all the praying needed.

We did not buy any lots from the Forest Lawn representative, but now some of the arrangements which would be needed were forced upon our attention. We were beginning to think about funeral arrangements and cemetery lots. However difficult and unpleasant it might be, we knew we had to face the terminal. We hoped we could do it as bravely as Mr. and Mrs. Joe Rozanc, people we had come to know through a mutual friend, Rose Holeman. The Rozancs' daughter, Debra Lynn, had leukemia, and our mutual sorrow brought us together in correspondence.

One day we received the following clipping in a letter from Rose:

DEBRA ROZANC DIES SUNDAY OF LEUKEMIA

Debra Lynn Rozanc, three-year-old daughter of

Mr. and Mrs. Joe A. Rozanc, died Sunday noon at Grand Haven Municipal Hospital.

Debra, who had been ill for seven months with acute leukemia, entered the hospital Sunday morning. She happily blew bubbles while sitting up in bed Saturday night and had enjoyed Christmas at home with the family.

Her health failed rapidly last week.

In her letter Rose wrote:

I went to see Mr. and Mrs. Rozanc last night. It is so hard to write about this to you, but they have expressed such a concern for you and want me to keep them informed. They are two brave people and definitely feel God very near to them now. They have asked me to tell you their prayers would continue for you and have pledged themselves to pray daily for scientists too.

There were several things of significance to me in this letter. First, we now added to our prayers for Danny the petition that when the time came for him to go it might be done with a minimum of difficulty for him. "O God," I prayed, "when it is time for Danny to leave us may it be that he too can be happily blowing bubbles." We had thought of Danny's terminal illness before, hoping it might not be unduly distressing for him. Now we brought this matter into specific prayer focus. We were also thankful that this letter revealed to us the bravery possible for parents by God's grace.

The letter concerning the Rozancs also pledged their daily prayers. My list of people who were praying each day that the cure or control for cancer might be found and that the families of cancer victims might be sustained was beginning to grow.

In the January, 1959, issue of *Today's Health,* Danny Thomas wrote of the St. Jude Hospital in Memphis. This hospital was the first leukemic research center in the nation with beds and laboratories. In the article Danny Thomas wrote: "I have always felt that the dollar philanthropist, the dime philanthropist, the kid-with-a-penny philanthropist is the most influential, most powerful and productive philanthropist in all the world. . . .

"If . . . we sat down," he went on, "and thought — really thought — about the importance of defeating catastrophic diseases, and then got the message across to 175 million Americans — and if only twenty-five per cent of them responded as dollar philanthropists, one-buck donors in the name of gratitude, think how many medical centers could be built."

This was exactly the principle I had in mind in regard to prayer. There were many who were willing to join in these worthy prayer objectives, and I came to know about many of them.

One of the most important considerations to us was that Danny's life, however brief it might be, would have value for others. This was one of the main reasons I began to write about our experiences during those days, hoping that they might prove of some help to somebody and in that way give Danny's short life an enlarged significance. This was true concerning a neighbor of ours in the valley. Who would have thought that a physically deficient child who died at an early age could become a blessing to millions of people? Yet that is just what happened when Dale Evans told her story in *Angel Unaware.*

Certainly Danny's life was going to have real significance for many people. Already he had strengthened the prayer life of many, and he had made many more sympathetic and understanding of their fellow-men. Alice and I discussed the possibility of other ways he might make a contribution to the welfare of others; we were thinking of such things as the donation of his eyes for someone who was blind.

In our school of affliction we were learning that Danny was not only a dear, sweet son to be enjoyed, but that his life was to have real worth. When it came time to return our son to the One who gave him to us, we could do so feeling He would say to Danny, "Well done, thou good and faithful servant." And we would be grateful we were loaned for a time such a precious and valuable possession of God. It occurred to me that since Danny was a loan, he should be returned graciously and thankfully when the time came. Why not? When someone returns a book I have loaned them, I receive a word of appreciation. I would be greatly surprised if it were returned with a complaint because I had not allowed one to keep it indefinitely. So we would try to return our son to the Giver.

In the February issue of *Today's Health* I found an article about a fellow resident of the San Fernando Valley which was of much help to me. Although the illness of their child was different, the experience of the parents was similar to ours. This article was also an encouragement to share our experiences with others in the hope they would be helped as we had been by reading the story of Jim and Nancy Storie and their daughter, Lisa, a Mongoloid infant.

Shortly after Lisa's birth, several disturbing indications began to worry the Stories. Specialists told them their child was mentally retarded. Lisa was taken to Children's Hospital, and after the tests were completed they were given an interview with the doctor. The article expressed our feelings exactly when it said of the Stories:

> Their emotions were contending in a nerve-wracking conflict between a desire to resolve the problem in the open where they might meet and attack it — and fear at what they were going to hear.
>
> Jim and Nancy Storie took their baby home in a stunned, unbelieving silence. At home, the reserve on which Nancy had been able to draw at the hospital collapsed under the weight of a terrible despondency.
>
> The two most difficult emotions Jim and Nancy had to overcome were self-pity and helplessness. These haven't been completely licked yet, but they are lessening daily.
>
> Now in the Storie household, doubt has changed to determination, shock to understanding, sorrow to hopefulness and — best of all — bewilderment to love. Jim and Nancy — and Kyle (their son), who knew it all along — now understand that love isn't dependent for its strength and power on attractive physical characteristics or mental brilliance, but rather on a deep-seated spiritual combination of affection, compassion, humility, hope, and kindness.

This article reveals the fact that problems of childhood illness cannot be met completely by medical treatment of the child. It is a problem of parents and their needed adjustments as well. Dr.

A. H. Parmalee, clinical professor of pediatrics at the U.S.C., pointed this out in an article (quoted in *Today's Health*): "Three steps for parents in solving the problem of the Mongoloid child are . . . first the acceptance of the fact that the infant is Mongoloid." This would also apply to any other illness. He goes on to say, "Next is acceptance of the responsibility of the child and his welfare. Finally comes the decision by the parents on the course of procedure they feel is best for them to follow." This plan, to restate it, means to face the facts, adjust to them, and do whatever needs doing in a thoughtful way.

As I had been a commercial pilot at one time, the story Marion L. Boling told in the *Reader's Digest* was a good illustration of facing reality and dealing with it in a constructive way. Under the title "The Best Hours of My Life" he told the story of how after 45 hours and 43 minutes he completed the longest nonstop flight without refueling ever made in a single-engine airplane. During the seven-thousand-mile trip from Manila to Pendleton, Oregon, he had much time for thought and reflection. At one point far out over the North Pacific it seemed he would have to ditch his plane because of severe icing. He wrote:

> Quickly I switched on the overhead light and reviewed my ditching instructions. Above them I had printed in big letters, "DON'T PANIC!" But this I had written in the security of our home. In the plane I was surrounded by weariness and the unknown. It was a time for prayer. As I had done every half hour, I begged God for guidance now to do the right thing. I asked Him to give me courage to meet

any emergency with dignity and grace — and then added, "*Thy* will be done."

This seemed to me a fine illustration of proper emergency procedure.

New evidence of science's advance against leukemia was coming to our attention. I was convinced that those of us who had pledged to pray daily that a cure or control for cancer might be found were taking a significant role in the medical advances we were hearing about.

I was finding a great deal more confidence in prayer — not only in prayers for cancer research, but in other areas as well. I would pray, for example, that the healing power of God's love would flow into and flood the life of someone in need, and I would have real assurance this was happening. From time to time, as occasion permitted, a verification of my assurance would be made known. Surely prayer is the most dynamic resource available to the human being.

I am sure that is just what Jesus intended to teach us.

Our personal and private prayers have power, but in corporate prayer, when minds and hearts are united in love and purpose, God's fuller power is often realized.

I could not possibly be more thankful than I was for the prayer cell to which I belonged at that time. There were four of us who met every Friday morning from eight until nine to pray. We experienced prayer to be an actual, palpable force, and the promise of Jesus, "When two or three are gathered together, there am I in the midst," became wonderfully true for us.

Our little prayer group started, as any other could start, when I became interested and felt the need for such a corporate prayer activity. (This was before Danny became ill.) I asked God to lead me to others with whom I might form a prayer fellowship. He did. Each of us in the group became deeply grateful for our prayer cell. Our lives were tremendously enriched spiritually, and we learned more of how to pray. We discovered how the Holy Spirit works, and it brought us peace and joy.

Our hour together followed somewhat the following pattern:

1. We had a short time of greeting and arranging our group into a circle.
2. We read a portion of the Bible.
3. We had a short discussion period on what had been read.
4. We had a brief time of testimony and witness. The discussion of the Bible selection usually led into this.
5. We mentioned certain specific objects which needed our prayers.
6. Then we prayed, going around the circle, each praying in turn.

In addition, we all promised to remember each of the other members of our prayer fellowship specifically by name in our prayers each day.

We may think of prayer, as one has suggested, as a bridge spanning the space between our weakness and God's strength. Over this bridge God walks into the lives of men and nations. Another has likened it to the lighting of candles which gradually expand the circle of His light.

Sunday, February 1, was Danny's fourth birthday. He had been waiting for this day for a long time. The day before he had asked us, "When is my birthday coming?" And we had told him, "Tomorrow." Early Sunday morning he came in our room asking, "Is this tomorrow?" We assured him it was. Before breakfast he opened his presents. He got a "Zorro" suit so he could pretend he was the same as the star of a favorite TV program. He also received a goldfish bowl with three fish. After his presents were opened, I asked him, "Danny, how old are you now?" He said, "I'm three years old." No," I said, "It's your birthday and you are now four." But he insisted he was only three "because," he explained, "we haven't had the birthday cake." After our noon dinner we had the cake with four candles, and then he was *officially* four. It took big puffs to blow out the candles, and I had a big wish for a little boy. In my prayer at the table I thanked God that our boy was with us.

In our Sunday morning services I was continuing expository studies in the book of Acts. On February 8 I preached from 9:32-43.

This paragraph brought me two valuable insights which proved to be of real help. A woman by the name of Dorcas had died. Her friends knew that Peter was in the neighborhood, and "they sent unto him two men, desiring him that he would not delay to come to them." How natural it was to send for a strong man. To hear that a strong man is coming is like hearing the angels sing. And, we found, there is always a strong man to send for! When the house is dark, we can send for Jesus. When life gives way in sudden weakness or in painful fear, we can send, in prayer, for Jesus.

I told my congregation, "But be not people who wait for a crisis in which to invite Jesus into your life. Send for Him today."

Jesus Christ was becoming more and more the center of our interest and affection, and what help, strength, and joy He brought to us! Praise His name!

Another insight into truth revealed in this paragraph of Scripture was suggested by the words of verse 39 where it tells us that "all the widows stood by him weeping, and shewing the coats and garments which Dorcas made, while she was with them." How is it that we like the coats and the garments even better when the seamstress is dead than when she was actually making them? That is a tender mystery of life. The little child's toy becomes infinitely precious when the tiny player can no longer play. And the two little shoes are the most precious property in the house when the little feet that wore them are put away in God's acre.

Eugene Field laid his finger on this truth when he wrote "Little Boy Blue":

> The little toy dog is covered with dust,
>   But sturdy and stanch he stands;
> And the little toy soldier is red with rust,
>   And his musket moulds in his hands.
> Time was when the little toy dog was new,
>   And the soldier was passing fair;
> And that was the time when our Little Boy Blue
>   Kissed them and put them there.

"Now, don't you go till I come," he said,
  "And don't you make any noise!"
So, toddling off to his trundle-bed,
  He dreamt of the pretty toys;
And, as he was dreaming, an angel song
  Awakened our Little Boy Blue –
Oh! the years are many, the years are long,
  But the little toy friends are true!

Ay, faithful to Little Boy Blue they stand,
  Each in the same old place,
Awaiting the touch of a little hand,
  The smile of a little face;
And they wonder, as waiting the long years through
  In the dust of that little chair,
What has become of our Little Boy Blue,
  Since he kissed them and put them there.

I used this poem in my sermon to illustrate the fact that the possessions of loved ones become so much more precious after their departure. Then I went on to say: "But let us love one another while we live! I do not speak a word against the sentiment which enlarges the actions of the dead, but I would speak a word on behalf of those who are sitting next to you and who are making your own house glad with their skillful fingers and their loving hearts."

In February I attended the meeting of the Board for Christian World Missions in Metuchen, New Jersey. My trip East brought something to my attention which was a real blessing and comfort. Because of the trip, my friend, the Reverend Floyd Menning, filled the pulpit of our church on the Sunday following my return. His text was Isaiah 55:8, 9: "For my thoughts are not your thoughts, neither are your ways my ways, saith the Lord. For as the heavens are higher than the earth, so are my ways higher than your ways, and my thoughts than your thoughts."

He began his sermon by saying that "suffering is the raw material with which to weave a garment of praise for God. There is no greater opportunity to praise God than when tragedy comes." He pointed out three important factors in God's dealing with man.

"First, God works on a different thought-level than man — 'For my thoughts are not your thoughts . . . saith the Lord.'

"We are like a man watching a parade, standing in the second row of spectators at street level. Such a man sees only one object at a time — that which is directly before him. The rest of the parade is obscured by the heads of the people to the right and to the left." But God, Reverend Menning told us, is like the observer who is on the roof of a building from which he sees the entire pageantry.

His second point was that "God works on a different technique level — 'Neither are your ways my ways, saith the Lord.'" God's ways are unique. Take, for example, His way of dealing with sin by taking a substitute to make satisfaction; it is so different from our technique that it becomes difficult for many to accept. Or, to use another example, the early Christians undoubtedly prayed for the removal of their archpersecutor Paul, but God changed him instead. Now when it comes to human suffering, God works on a different technique level, using suffering to work perfection.

The third point Reverend Menning made concerning the problem of suffering was that "God works on a different time level." He quoted the text from 2 Peter which states that "One day is with the Lord as a thousand years, and a thousand years as one day."

He mentioned that about the only contribution of this age to civilization is speed and noise. I knew what he was talking about — I had just returned from New York City on a jet plane! God's ways and workings are often painfully and irritatingly slow for our impatient day.

He closed with an illustration of a doctor who had attended Winona Lake Bible Conference at the same time Reverend Menning had been there. They had learned the chorus "My Lord Knows the Way Through the Wilderness, All I Have to Do Is Follow." Shortly after the doctor returned home, his wife and three of his four children died of polio. He wrote back to Winona Lake that the little chorus had pulled him through. I knew from personal experience what that little chorus could do. When I had passed through the "slough of despond" which kept me from my pulpit for several weeks a few years before this, I found great help from the same simple chorus which was such a blessing to the doctor.

The preaching of Floyd Menning was a real blessing to me that morning. What he said was true, and I believed it. It was helpful and encouraging and yet — the gnawing agony that my son had an incurable disease never left. It was there, always there; like the grain of wood, it showed up through all the rest of my daily activities. It was there when I would go into Danny's room at night and stand and watch him sleeping either on his back with his little mouth open in peaceful slumber or turned over on his side, his two hands under his cheek like a little cherub. It was there when I washed off the grime of active play from his chubby cheeks and hands before a meal. It was there when he called out, "Come on, dad, let's play cowboys!" All the philosophizing, all the theologizing, all the rationalizing wouldn't change the hard, cold fact that in Danny's system lay a rebellion to life, a gangster outbreak of misplaced cells. Again and again the bewildering stupefication which rose in our protesting hearts when we first learned the nature of Danny's illness came to taunt and haunt. God was a "very present help in trouble," but those were, nevertheless, unhappy days.

We were pleased to have my sister and brother-in-law, Freida and Art VanderPloeg, visit us. Our fellowship with these dear ones had been close and wonderful through the years. They had done much for us. (For example, they had made possible a trip I took to Palestine.) Art is a mortician, and I had planned to seek his advice concerning the matter of Danny's burial. He approached me about it.

One day while sight-seeing we drove past one of the many spacious funeral homes of Los Angeles. "Bern," he said, "we hope the time will never come, but if and when it should, have you thought about what arrangements you would want?"

"I have been thinking about that," I told him, "and I would like your advice."

Art promised to check with a few funeral homes concerning costs and other arrangements. One of the first decisions we would need to make would be the place of burial.

Alice had said, "Since Danny was born and lived all his life in California, I think it should be here." On the other hand, the residence of a minister is subject to change; if we left there would be no relative to visit the grave. If he were buried in my hometown or Alice's hometown, this would not be the case.

One day while Art and Freida were with us, we drove to a beautiful little cemetery near us, nestled in the hills which surround our valley. It was a quiet, restful place where the body of the daughter of our friends Dorothy and Ken Baird was buried. Danny was with us the day we drove through this cemetery. He had no idea at all, of course, of the nature of our visit or even the purpose of the cemetery. But Alice and I both felt an eerie cloud of apprehension stifling us. We were both relieved as the car took us through the gates and away from the place, not wanting to think that we might be returning, but unable to ignore the possibility.

Chapter 4

A visit with Roy Rogers and Dale Evans, the dream of every child in those days, came true for Danny. On a Tuesday morning a busy schedule was interrupted by a phone call from the Rogers' ranch. Roy and Dale, whom I had previously met and who had visited our church, had heard of Danny's illness and wondered if he would like to come over the next morning to see the ranch. What boy wouldn't? I didn't want to appear over-eager, but I said "Yes" as quickly as I could.

We didn't tell Danny that night for fear the excitement might keep him awake. The next morning about an hour before we left, I said, "Danny, how would you like to see Roy Rogers and Dale Evans?"

Danny said, "I saw Roy Rogers on TV last night."

"I mean, how would you like to visit them on their ranch? We're going there this morning."

He looked at me with the most wide-eyed amazement I've ever seen on a child. His one word was "Really???"

Yes, it was really so. Alice had polished his cowboy boots the evening before, and his cowboy shirt was cleaned and pressed.

"Is it time to go yet?" he asked.

"No, it isn't time to go yet, Danny."

"It sure takes a long time before it's time to go," he complained.

But soon we were in our red and white station wagon, driving the couple of miles to our gracious neighbors who had extended this kind invitation.

We drove up the winding lane to their house which was nestled in the hills on the west end of the San Fernando Valley. We parked the car, and Dale opened the door into their spacious and comfortable living room.

Roy came in and greeted us, and Danny watched in fascination as Roy took one of Danny's guns and gave an exhibition of fancy gun-twirling. There were pictures and statues of horses to capture the attention of Danny.

As we talked over a leisurely cup of coffee, Dale expressed the feeling that one of the major problems the Christian church must face is the problem of suffering. "You know," she said, "the Cross tells us that there is no spiritual progress without pain."

In their living room was an alcove for prayer and worship. Here was a place to kneel in prayer before an open Bible, and the place was well-worn. On the wall was the colorful and delightful picture by Sallman of Christ carrying the lost sheep. Dale's entire conversation was saturated with spiritual insights and centered about Christ.

Roy took Danny, Alice, and me into his den. Here we saw the impressive trophies of his recent safari in Africa. Danny also saw his guns, trophies, pictures, and other mementos which filled the room to overflowing.

I took a picture of Danny with Roy's arm around him; it is a treasured keepsake of our visit with these famous people. Another is a picture of Danny with Roy's horse, Trigger. A third is a jacket they put on Danny, a real western one with leather fringes on the arm and bottom and Roy Rogers' name inside. But most important of all is the memory of these gracious Christian people who gave a moment of delight to our little boy.

Shortly after Danny first became ill, our church established a blood bank with the Red Cross. Early in his illness he needed blood and would again, we were told, near the end. The Red Cross told us that a reserve of twenty pints was needed before we could begin drawing blood from our bank. By the first of March we had only nine pints in our bank. Some had gone to give blood but were unable to because of a blood deficiency. Others had neglected or forgotten. Still others had gone but found the Red Cross unable to accommodate all donors. It was understandable that this one facility for blood collection, which was open only five hours every other week and which had to serve the entire valley with a population of over 800,000 people, would be unable to accommodate all those willing to donate blood. It disturbed me to know that there were people needing blood and that there were people who would contribute blood but who were prevented by inadequate accommodation.

I called the Red Cross and asked them about this. I was told that the reason adequate provision for the collection of blood could not be made was because of lack of funds made available to the Red Cross by donation.

This answer did not seem to me to be sufficient reason for shutting off the flow of this life-giving liquid.

On Sunday morning in March I visited Danny's Sunday school department. Danny was sitting with the other boys and girls and his happy face and alert eyes spoke of his full participation and enjoyment of the hour. He was wearing his new brown suit. A pair of my cuff links buttoned his shirt cuffs, and a sporty bow tie rode well on his collar. He looked so much a part of this happy group of four-year-olds, so much a part and yet so terribly different from them.

On March 11 we took Danny to Children's Hospital for his monthly checkup with Dr. Brubaker. Alice and I had a premonition that all was not well. Several things suggested this. Danny had had two slight nosebleeds during the previous week, he was more irritable, and he had two or three bruises on his legs. His general condition just did not seem as good as it had been. However, we thought that perhaps that was because he had a siege of the mumps (he called them the "humps") the previous week.

Dr. Brubaker made his examination. He told us the result of the blood test was good — the best it had yet been. His physical examination revealed nothing which suggested any change in Danny's remission. But we had to wait until the next day for the results of the all-important bone-marrow test.

The next day the doctor called to tell us the results. It was not good. The bone-marrow test showed the first indications of the drug losing its ability to keep Danny in remission. We had hoped with the doctor that the first drug would keep Danny in remission for some time longer than it then appeared it would. The doctor asked us to come in the next week when, after examination, he would decide whether Danny should be switched to the second of the three groups of drugs used. As I faced the end of the first third of Danny's life expectancy, my spirit drooped like a wilted flower and I prayed for strength.

Danny had named the three fish he got for his birthday Danny, Dorothy, and Zorro. The day after we got the adverse report from the doctor, the fish named Danny died.

The next week we again went to Children's Hospital for Danny's checkup to determine the effectiveness of the drug he was taking. Dr. Brubaker was wearing his cowboy boots, as he had promised Danny he would.

The familiar procedure began. First the nurse took a sample of his blood — Danny was taking *this* in stride by now. Next, there was a half-hour wait while the blood was tested and the doctor examined the results. Then came the physical examination by the doctor — weight, eyes, mouth, liver, and spleen. Usually this was the end of the examination, but today, as sometimes was needed, a bone-marrow test was taken. This Danny didn't take in his stride.

His campaign to escape would begin with a question, "Daddy, why don't we go now?" Or, "Daddy, I don't want a mosquito bite today!" We called the bone puncture necessary for the test a mosquito bite. His resistance would grow stronger after the doctor was ready for the minor surgery. I held his head and arms, one nurse held him at the waist, and another held his feet.

I wanted him to lie quietly, but I couldn't help admiring the drive and fight he put up to resist what surely must have been to him unreasonable torture.

The results of the test were not known before we left, and the doctor promised to call later. Before we left, he gave us a small supply of the new drug which Danny would have to take if the test indicated its need. The pills were very small, and Danny would have to take eight of them a day. They were also very bitter. And they were expensive, each pill costing forty cents. The doctor also told us that this drug would greatly increase Danny's appetite. He would gain weight and his face would become puffy. We would need to reduce his salt intake as much as possible. And four times a day he would have to take potassium acetate which his body would be discharging too rapidly as an effect of this drug.

Saturday morning Alice came to the new church where I was working with other members of the congregation in cleaning. Although it was still incomplete we were going to hold services there the next Sunday, Palm Sunday. When my heart was heavy, as it was then, I found that doing something active helped to soothe and assuage the burden.

"The doctor called," Alice said happily, "and Danny is still in complete remission." There was an unaccountable fluctuation in the test, he had told her, but the later test showed complete remission. It was a bright day for us.

Now I knew what God was saying to me in a verse of Scripture I had read that morning: "O thou afflicted one, tossed with tempest, and not comforted, behold, I will lay thy stones with fair colours, and lay thy foundations with sapphires" (Isa. 54:11).

On April 17, the day following Danny's regular monthly check-up, Dr. Brubaker called. "Yesterday's bone-marrow test shows that Danny now needs a different drug."

Danny had had the flu for a few days previous to the examination which revealed this change. He was irritable, his appetite was gone, he had a fever, and he woke up frequently during the night. But what gave us the most concern was the fact that his legs were tender and sensitive, and he had difficulty in walking. It reminded us of the initial indications of the disease. Alice and I had exchanged concerned looks. Now our fears were confirmed. Danny was beginning the second mile of his "three-mile journey." That evening we began the second of the three drugs used.

The doctor told us the last two drugs would be given alternately at six-week intervals, instead of using each drug for its maximum duration. There were two reasons for this.

In the first place, Prednisone created an over-active appetite. We might expect Danny to eat like an adult, and his body would have a tendency to absorb liquid so that there would be a real problem with obesity. By alternating the last two drugs this would be reduced.

But even more, it was a matter of strategy in this grim game with death. Before the disease could find a way past the drug, it would be confronted with a new drug, whose secrets of defense it would then attempt to overcome. But before it could, the defense would again be changed. Each time, however, the disease would be less confused. Its relentless energy would never fag until it had accomplished its grisly mission.

But we would give it the toughest battle possible. Just like Danny fought the bone-marrow test with a determination I admired, so we would fight the invader of his body.

We had now walked the first mile with Danny. It had been five months since we learned of his incurable disease. Five months during which, by God's grace, we had walked this mile with some serenity. When we began this via dolorosa it was with confusion and despair. The way of suffering seemed impossible.

One source of great strength and help was the daily communion with God in my "quiet time." Here, while reading His word and talking with Him in prayer, I found:

> *There is a place of quiet rest*
> *Near to the heart of God.*

Again and again God had a message for me. For example, one day as I read from Matthew 6 (RSV), God showed me a fourfold method of facing and overcoming fear and anxiety:

1. *Learn that anxiety is useless.* Jesus asked, "And which of you by being anxious can add one cubit to his span of life?" (v. 27). Anxiety is a supreme example of wasted effort.

2. *We have a heavenly Father,* Jesus taught us. It is not as if we are adrift in a hostile world. God in mercy, love, and care has searched us out and will never leave us. Jesus said, "Your heavenly Father knows" (v. 32). Isn't that enough?

3. *Anxiety is overcome when one is busy* — and not just busy with anything, but busy with the things of God's kingdom. "Seek first his kingdom, and his righteousness" (v. 33). The greatest personal problem most of us have is that we are self-centered. This is an accomplishment of sin. This must be changed to a Christ-centeredness.

4. The fourth blow to be dealt fear and anxiety is to *live each day and only each day.* Why borrow tomorrow's troubles and add them to today's? Jesus said, "Therefore do not be anxious about tomorrow, for tomorrow will be anxious for itself." Then with a world of common sense and help He added, "Let the day's own trouble be sufficient for the day" (v. 34).

This was the kind of help I was finding daily in the Word of God.

Because of Danny's illness we were hearing from others with grave personal problems who needed help, too. A former member of the church my father pastored wrote me, part of which I quote:

I can feel for you extremely as we too have a son of 14 with an incurable disease. He has *lupus erythematosis*, a blood disease which is similar to that of your son in many respects. The difference is that the red corpuscles eat the white ones. He also has to stay out of all natural light because light and sun would hasten his death. We keep our home dark at all times which makes it a very small world for us. He feels reasonably well most of the time. I should have said "bearably" because he is really never himself. Then at times he has severe joint pains and swellings which go with the disease. It is a most pitiful and heart-breaking condition. He is a handsome young man. He has an inquiring mind which makes him seek an answer to *why* he is sick and is God love? Can He be trusted? He was a real Christian and much interested in Christianity before he took sick. He spent much time studying the Bible. The summer before he took sick he memorized 500 verses of Scripture. When asked by other children why he did it (mockingly oftentimes) he would hold Christ high. He also told me that by learning these verses now he could use them when he became a minister. At first after his ailment he felt as strong in his faith as ever. Now he feels that his fervent prayers have not been answered and what's the use.

Here was a double tragedy. Not only were the parents going through a sorrowful experience, but the boy, being fourteen, was old enough to realize the situation and so the physical discomfort was accompanied by the mental anguish as well. Our Danny was young enough to be spared this additional burden.

During all of these months I did a great deal of reading, thinking, and praying concerning the subject of divine or supernatural healing.

I find that a teaching has grown up which says that anyone may be supernaturally healed of any sickness at any time if certain conditions are met. I do not believe that such sweeping conclusions are warranted, but there are, I believe, some conclusions which can be made concerning this matter.

We know of two times when there is no sickness — first in the Garden of Eden before the Fall (Gen. 1:31), and the other in heaven (Rev. 21:4). Between these two we have sickness. Also, between these two we have sin. The first is the result of the second. This connection may be personal or impersonal. That is, people may be sick because of their personal sin, and it may be equally true that their sickness is in no way related to personal sin.

The second conclusion, as I understand it, is that all healing is divine. There are many healing agencies in the world. These, I believe, are used by God to effect healing. But it is His power working through these agencies that actually brings the desired results.

In addition to this, God, without human means, brings healing. Can God do this today? Need we ask that? God planned the intricacies of the circulatory system with its twenty-five trillion blood corpuscles. God fashioned the human eye with its retina containing two million rods and cones. Of course, God can heal.

Is God interested in healing? God is more interested in the affairs of men than in anything else. God loves, cares, and will heal. The life and work of Jesus Christ is abundant evidence of this. It might be pointed out here that about two-thirds of the healings performed by Christ were in answer to the expressed faith of those who were ill. (For example: Matt. 9:20-22; 15:21-28; and Mark 2:1-5.) Fully a third of the recorded healings have no reference to such faith. (Such as John 11:1-44; Luke 22:50, 51; and Acts 3:1-11.)

But by far the most important consideration is that God does not always heal. God *can* always heal, but God does not *always* will to heal. The outstanding example is Paul. Paul had a physical difficulty, and Galatians 6:11 and 4:15 suggest it may have been eye trouble of some kind. But God's will for him (see 2 Cor. 12:7-10) was that he should not be healed. And there are other similar New Testament situations (2 Tim. 4:20; Phil. 2:25-30; and 1 Tim. 5:23).

There is no doubt in my mind that although God can heal, it is not always His will to heal. And the reason for this may often be known. Sometimes it is a way in which God's kingdom and His glory are enhanced. We are taught in Hebrews 12:9-11: "Furthermore we have had fathers of our flesh which corrected us, and we gave them reverence: shall we not much rather be in subjection unto the Father of spirits, and live? For they verily for a few days chastened us after their own pleasure; but he for our profit, that we might be partakers of his holiness. Now no chastening for the present seemeth to be joyous, but grievous: nevertheless afterward it yieldeth the peaceable fruit of righteousness unto them which are exercised thereby."

Sickness is often a teacher. Many a Christian has learned the ways of God during illness. Human compassion and understanding are often learned in illness.

Sickness may glorify God by revealing His grace. A Christian's testimony really counts when given in a time of trouble. Unbelievers can be mightily stirred when Christians live for God in times of pain and tears.

The teaching of the present-day healing movement is that when Christ died He not only bore our sins but took our sickness as well. So just as surely as faith in Christ means forgiveness of sins, it also means healing from sickness. This I cannot accept. I believe healing is in the Atonement, but as a potential — the same as heaven is in the Atonement, but to be received later.

In no way do I doubt God's ability; in no way do I doubt that sometimes it is His will to heal. I did pray for Danny's healing, just as I pray for the healing of others who are ill. There are many Christians alive and well today who speak of God's healing. I believe a larger place should be given today in the church of Jesus Christ to Christ's ministry of physical healing. But I do not believe that healing is for everyone or that a lack of healing signifies a lack of faith.

One day Alice said to me, "Danny has certainly had a happy life." It was true that he had. Every day was a day of play and happiness for him. He was a born "player." He had a vivid imagination which enabled him to turn the everyday world into a magic kingdom of make-believe. Coupled with this was a blithe spirit. He would giggle and laugh at the slightest provocation. He enjoyed hearing a joke — and telling one. For example, instead of saying the customary "hot-diggidy-dog," he would say "hot-diggidy-cow" or "cat" and then giggle with delight.

He was beginning to show the signs of obesity that the doctors had told us would be a side effect of the drug he was taking. His body, always sturdy and husky, was now becoming rolypoly. If it were not for its sinister cause, it would have been rather amusing.

Danny especially loved the swimming pool. Every day he was swimming, and he could swim like a fish. He had no fear as he plunged from the diving board into the eight-and-a-half feet of water. With huge flippers on his feet and goggles over his eyes, he looked like a miniature frogman as he expertly made his way across the water.

Danny loved life and he was happy. Weary from a day of play, he would sink into untroubled sleep. Through the night his sleep was sound. Next morning he would awaken grinning and bouncing, ready for another day of happy play.

The newspapers of May 27 reported:

> The death rate from leukemia has been increasing faster than that of any other form of cancer except lung cancer but medical progress has

increased the life span of the leukemia victim, the American Cancer Society said today.

The society said in a special report on the disease that the leukemia death rate among males of all ages has risen from 2.5 per 100,000 population in 1930 to 7.4 in 1956. Among females, the death rate increased from 1.8 to 5.1 during the same period.

I had been asked several times if leukemia was on the increase. I didn't know it was until I read the news item in the paper. Now that I knew it was, the first question which came to mind was, "Why?" Could it be the contamination of the air because of A-bomb testing? This was the contention of some.

It was common knowledge, of course, that lung cancer too was on the increase. And the reason was obvious. E. Cuyler Hammond, director of statistical research for the American Cancer Society, stated that the death rate from lung cancer was roughly ten times as high among average cigarette smokers as among nonsmokers. He also stated that the lung cancer death rate of the two-or-more-packs-a-day cigarette smokers was roughly sixty times as high as among nonsmokers. But there was no such obvious answer concerning leukemia, whose death rate gained more than any other cancer.

Danny had now been on Prednisone for six weeks. A test made by Dr. Brubaker showed that he was still in complete remission. Now Danny was switched to Methotrexate. This drug would decrease his appetite, and it was easier to take. Danny would need only 1½ tablets, a dosage determined by his weight. He would not need any of the other medicines, and he could again use salt.

Since Danny became ill I had become increasingly aware and concerned that the patient, not merely the disease, be treated. Support for this thesis came from a rather unexpected source: a translation I read of a Russian professor's notebook which emphasized old-fashioned sympathy for the patient.

We often tend to concentrate our attention on some organ or other and to speak of its diseases, although pathological physiology has shown us that in the disrupted function of an individual organ there is always a response by the body as a whole. This unity of the body also includes the psychic sphere.

The doctor is making a great mistake if, in examining the patient, he confines himself . . . to writing a prescription and does not concern himself with the patient's mental state.

The present-day Soviet doctor knows very well that it is of the utmost importance to sympathize with the patient whom he is treating. The "impersonal" doctor must be abolished, and the sooner the better, if we want to put our treatment of the workers on the highest possible level of quality, particularly in the early stages of an illness.*

I wish all men of medical science could hear and would heed the words of this Soviet professor. Our doctors were of this disposition, which was to be our benefit.

This need for a person-to-person relationship, rather than a person-to-disease relationship, came to my attention in another way about this time.

*Dr. G. S. Pondoev, *Notes of a Soviet Doctor*, Consultants Bureau.

In helping a family with a delinquent boy, I had occasion to talk to the headmaster of the school for boys where we brought this boy to be enrolled. This man, well-trained and experienced in the behavior patterns of teen-agers, told me that the difference between a boy in trouble and one not in trouble was largely a matter of verbalization.

"The boy who can talk out his inner feelings," he told me, "rarely has difficulty. On the other hand, the boy who cannot verbalize, for reasons within himself or because he has no one with whom he can share his inner feelings, acts out his feelings often in untoward acts which run afoul of accepted social relationships."

In other words, every person needs two things: one, the ability to express his inner feelings; and two, one to whom these feelings can be expressed. Here the Bible is of inestimable help. It helps its reader to understand and articulate his inner feelings. Again and again as one reads these words he spontaneously exclaims, "Why, that's just exactly how I feel, only I couldn't put it into words." In literature, it is said, there are but thirty-six dramatic situations on which all drama and literature are based. Goethe and others have tried to develop more than these basic dramatic situations but without success. Similarly there are but twenty-six letters in the English language from which all writing is made. All Occidental music comes from seven tones on the musical scale. Life is like that, too. There are certain invariable and unchangeable basic inner feelings — the Bible helps us to recognize and verbalize these.

The Bible also shows the One to whom anyone may go. It is to Jesus Christ. "Seeing that we have a great High Priest who has entered the inmost Heaven, Jesus the Son of God, let us hold firmly to our faith. For we have no superhuman High Priest to whom our weaknesses are unintelligible — he himself has shared fully in all our experiences of temptation, except that he never sinned. Let us therefore approach the throne of grace with fullest confidence, that we may receive mercy for our failures and grace to help in the hour of need" (Heb. 4:14-16, *Phillips*).

One of the greatest of the ministries of men is performed when they provide an ear and a heart for others. Pastors, parents, teachers, and many others little realize the significance of their contribution to others when they are willing to listen with sympathy and love.

God was teaching us many things through our son and his illness. Danny was a constant source of delight to us. His personality was so pleasant and agreeable that we dreaded the thought of losing him.

Danny was, at this time, on his third drug. The doctor had warned us that it might produce sores in his mouth. After a few days they did appear. Danny told us about them. That night when he prayed, he included this sentence: "Dear Jesus, that you will make the sores in my mouth better." Not, "will you make them better?" but "you will." His confidence in his friend Jesus was beautiful.

But there was a fascinating impishness about him, too. One evening we were lying together on the bed. I was reading, while Danny was looking at pictures in a book. As he was paging along he tore one page slightly.

"Dad," he said, "I tore a page. I'm sorry." Then he kissed me to prove it.

I was pleased with fatherly pride that he acknowledged an error and was sorry for it, a pride that was to be punctured a moment later. We went on reading for a few moments, then:

"Dad."

"Yes, Danny."

"Do you know why I said, 'I'm sorry'?"

"No. Why?"

"If I say 'I'm sorry,' then I don't get punished," he explained.

The battle for mastery of the disease which had stricken our son continued, and no one watched it with more interest or greater concern than Alice and I did. We, with our friends, were praying daily that the trail being blazed to mastery over cancer might soon reach its destination.

Chapter 5

We spent our vacation that year in my boyhood hometown of Sioux Center, Iowa. Here with my mother and my sister and her family we rested, played, and read. Danny soon became well known in the little village. One reason was that at four years of age he became the youngest child, according to the lifeguards, to ever jump off the fifteen-foot tower at the local swimming hole.

While on vacation, I received a telephone call from a member of our church, my good friend John Slagter. A sudden tragedy had come into their lives.

His wife Jean had been working in the kitchen. Their eight-month-old baby was munching a cracker while sitting in her high chair.

Jean stepped outside for just a few minutes to change the water sprinkler. When she came back, her baby was dead. She had choked on the cracker.

When we came home from vacation, Alice and I went to visit this spiritually mature couple.

"John," I said, "tell me what was the single, most comforting and helpful thought you had during this tragedy?"

Without a moment's hesitation he answered, "It is the assurance from God's Word that we will be reunited."

This is the promise of the Word. John was restating the same comfort David had found. David's son had been ill, and he saw his servants whispering. He asked, "Is the child dead?" They answered, "He is dead."

Before the death David had fasted and wept. When he learned of the death, he washed, changed his clothes, ate, and went to God's house to worship. His servants felt that this was very strange behavior.

David's explanation was, "While the child was yet alive, I fasted and wept: for I said, Who can tell whether God will be gracious to me, that the child may live? But now he is dead, wherefore should I fast? Can I bring him back again? I shall go to him, but he shall not return to me."

This, to John and Jean, who had never had a major tragedy in their lives before, was their single, greatest source of comfort and help.

While we were conversing, John suddenly said something which was a direct answer to a question I had raised when Danny first became ill. His statement was, "We will never regret we had Karen for eight months." Earlier I had wondered, as I have recorded in chapter 1, which would be better — to have a loved one for a short time only to lose him through sickness and death, or never to have had him at all. After much struggle I had come to the same conclusion John had expressed.

While we were in their home, John and Jean shared with me a printed sermon preached by Dr. E. W. Palmer of the Judson Baptist Church, Oak Park, Illinois. It was the first message by this pastor after his wife and sixteen-year-old son had passed away within months of each other due to results of an automobile accident. His text was 2 Corinthians 12:9, "My grace is sufficient for thee." His testimony was, "I believe in the sufficiency of God's grace."

These friends had brought me comfort and courage on the afternoon I went to comfort them. Their mature, spiritual response to the crushing blow which had come into their lives reminded me of a poem which had come to my attention. Two young teen-agers, active in Youth for Christ, had been killed in a tragic automobile accident which had shocked the Christian community in Los Angeles.

The morning of the tragedy the young girl had prayed with a friend, "Lord, help me to live this day for Thee as though it were my last day here on earth."

That afternoon, just hours before the accident, the boy had played and sung a gospel song in a parade celebrating a community event in a neighboring city. His song had been, "Bye and Bye When the Morning Comes."

The poem quoted here was on the memorial folder for these two Christian teen-agers.

"I'll lend you for a time a child of Mine," He said;
"For you to love the while he lives, and mourn for when he's dead.
It may be six or seven years or only two or three,
But will you, till I call him back, take care of him for Me?
He'll bring his charms to gladden you, and should his stay be brief;
You'll have his lovely memories as solace for your grief.
I cannot promise he will stay, since all from earth return,
But there are lessons taught down there I want this child to learn.
I've looked this wide world over in search for teachers true,
And from the throngs that crown life's loves I have selected you.
Now will you give him all your love, nor think the labor vain,
Nor hate Me when I come to call to take him back again?"
I fancied that I heard them say, "Dear Lord thy will be done,
For all the joy the child shall bring, the risk of grief we'll run.
We'll shelter him with tenderness, we'll love him while we may,
And for the happiness we've known forever grateful stay.
But should the angels call for him much sooner than we've planned,
We'll brave the bitter grief that comes and try to understand."

The days of vacation gave me the time for meditation and Bible study which helped me formulate, crystallize, and put into words a philosophy of life adequate to meet days of darkness.

There were two questions to which I directed my attention. The first: Is there a purpose served in suffering? And the second: How does one live with suffering? By "suffering" I had in mind any physical, mental, emotional, social, or financial problem, difficulty, or adversity which came into life.

I knew that in dealing with the problem of suffering I was dealing with one of the greatest mysteries under the sun. It is a universal problem, knowing no economic, educational, racial, or religious barriers.

First, I asked myself, "Is there a purpose in suffering?" I did believe there was an "eternal purpose" (Eph. 3:11) in all things. One reason why I felt this must be true was because of the Cross. Here from the greatest of all sufferings flowed the greatest of all blessings!

The purpose of our sufferings must be great to exact the costly price of heartache, sorrow, and tears. I was determined to find their purpose. Perhaps many were paying the price (suffering) without receiving the value (recognizing and achieving the purpose). I was determined to receive that for which I was paying so costly a price.

My quest was successful. As I pondered these things, I began to see certain valuable purposes born from suffering.

One purpose sometimes achieved by suffering is the salvation of sinners. If it had not been for husks, hunger, and hogs, the prodigal would never have returned home. In a time of pain and death the thief on the Cross found the Lord.

Suffering has brought many a prodigal home. One was Abraham Poljak, a Jew persecuted under Hitler. He wrote:

> I am one of the Jews who escaped from Germany. I thank God for all the strokes with which I was driven from darkness to light. It is better that we arrive beaten and bloody at the glorious goal than that we decay happily and contentedly in darkness. As long as things were all right with us, we did not know anything of God, anything of salvation of our souls and the world beyond. Hitler's arrows and our misery led us to reality. We have lost our earthly home, but have found the heavenly one. We have lost our economic support, but have won the friendship of the ravens of Elijah. In the bitter ways of emigration we have found Jesus, the Riches of the World.

A second purpose sometimes accomplished by suffering is the correction of God's children.

Job, in whose life is found the greatest instruction in suffering to be found outside of Jesus Christ, expresses this truth, "When He has tried me I shall come forth as gold."

Anyone who cannot say "I am willing to serve God out of a pure, unselfish love, and not for what I may get out of it" is in need of such correction. Suffering has a way of throwing the Christian completely on the mercy of God.

As I thought of suffering being a testing of our devotion to God and a correction for straying, there came to my mind the fact that God, too, in a sense, was being tested! God has said, "My grace is sufficient for you" (2 Cor. 12:9). In the life of suffering Christians, this is tested. We have the plain picture of this in the life of Job. What a risk, you might say, God was taking.

Paul writes, "We are made a spectacle unto the world, and to angels and to men" (1 Cor. 4:9). The word "spectacle" literally means "theater." God's ability to sustain and maintain is being demonstrated in every difficulty of life.

As a Christian these questions came to me: Am I a vindication of my God? Am I a proof of His grace? Is there in me a demonstration that God is able?

A third purpose, which had previously been understood, was that suffering brings a compassion for others and an ability and desire to comfort. This ability to serve is perfected in the crucible of suffering.

Annie J. Flint put it in words of exquisite loveliness and powerful truth:

> *O Christ! Who once has seen Thy visioned beauty —*
> *He counts all gain but loss,*
> *And other things are naught if he may win Thee*
> *And share with Thee Thy cross.*
> *And he on whom its shadow once has fallen,*
> *Walks quietly and apart;*
> *He holds the master-key of joy and sorrow*
> *That open every heart.*
> *The burdened souls that pass him on the highway*
> *Turn back to take his hand,*
> *And murmur low, with tear-wet eyes of anguish,*
> *You know — you understand.*

I would rather spend five minutes with a humble saint of God who has needed and received God's comfort than hear all the logic and words of theologians, philosophers, or orators who have not. They just do not have the "master key."

G. Campbell Morgan tells of an incident which illustrates this factor. He had a young friend who was brought to God through Dr. Morgan's ministry. He became a minister, and one day Dr. Morgan went to hear him preach. "His sermon," Dr. Morgan writes, "was wonderful, brilliant, sparkling in eloquence." When they returned home, Dr. Morgan asked his wife what she thought of the sermon. Her reply was, "It was wonderful; but it will be better when he has had some trouble." Dr. Morgan did not hear him preach again until after the young preacher had stood by the side of a grave and his heart had been smitten. Dr. Morgan's comment was, "Oh, the difference!"

Somehow it is through the hour of sorrow that we become instruments able to convey to people the message of God that heals and helps. I do not think that any should seek the pathway of suffering, but I think that the person who is in the midst of buffeting may know that by such processes the truth of God will become living and powerful.

The other question on which I meditated and sought answer from God's Word was: How does one face or live with suffering? To this question, too, God gave me answers of remarkable clearness and help.

The first step was to commit one's life to the Lord. God had spoken to me in Psalm 37:5,

"Commit thy way unto the Lord; trust also in him; and he shall bring it to pass."

I once read of a missionary who was confronted by the unbelieving captain of the ship which was taking him to a foreign shore. The captain asked, "What if you die?" The missionary's answer was, "I have already done that." It was the truth expressed by Paul in Galatians 2:20, "I am crucified with Christ: nevertheless I live: yet not I, but Christ liveth in me."

God was teaching me to say, "It isn't my life — it is His." Recognizing that it is His relieves me of the responsibility of control; my responsibility is one of surrender. I need not figure out the future or attempt to manipulate it, but confidently I give myself to Him and His plan.

This, it seemed to me, was the first step in living with suffering.

The second step was to live just one day at a time. It was Jesus who taught us not to add tomorrow's trouble to today when He said, "Sufficient unto the day is the evil thereof" (Matt. 6:34).

One day I was talking in my study with an alcoholic who had a sincere desire to resist drink. He said to me, "When I think of all those days ahead when I must go without drink — I can't do it." I asked him, "Do you think God is able to keep you for the next hour?" I told him to live just the next hour without drink by God's help. "Do not borrow the trouble from all the hours beyond that," I said. This was the way he began his total abstinence — just one short period at a time. Today he is cured.

Again and again there came to my mind thoughts of the final sickness, then the death, then the funeral, then the burial. But these things had not happened yet, so why should I already bear their pain and agony? "Sufficient unto the day is the evil thereof." And sufficient unto the day is the grace thereof!

The third step I learned from God's Word was not to allow emotions, unaided, to call the signals. We usually live and act according to how we feel. If we feel depressed, we will live and act dejectedly. If we feel irritated, our actions reveal this. In other words our feelings determine our course of action. Emotions are in control. But it need not be this way. Instead we can live and act positive — regardless of whether we feel like it or not!

I have experimented with this and found amazing results. Suppose I feel miserable inside. If I let these feelings take control, I will be grouchy, irritable, and difficult. But if I refuse to allow my emotions to dictate my action and instead act pleasantly and serve others with kindness, I will have served my better judgment rather than my emotions. But — and here comes the amazing thing — it won't be long before my emotions begin to match my actions! I have always thought that emotions control actions, and they usually do, but they don't have to — actions can control emotions.

The fourth and by far the most significant step involved in facing suffering is the putting of Jesus Christ in the very center of life. A young mother came to know Jesus Christ as her Lord and Savior in our church. Previously, while self was at the center of life, she had had many fears and great emotional difficulties. Her testimony, spontaneously written and given to me, is an adequate illustration and explanation of the point I am trying to make here.

I feel as if every pain I've ever had, every joy I've ever felt, every thought I've every thought has been to bring me to this humble place at the feet of the Lord looking up to Him for every answer. It has taken much to humble me, who thought the world should be mine, whose life was make-up, clothes, cute things to say, and a fabulous home. Then, as an afterthought, came my husband and children; then, way behind them, others trailed. My only thoughts at that time were how well liked I was. Old self is dying hard and is still gasping for breath, but by the grace of the Lord, it is dying. Now God is my reason for everything. For the first time in my life I really love other people. Now I can relax all tension and anxiety in the Lord. My old fears and new ones will still come but as they do I will claim freedom in the name of Jesus — and wherever He takes me I will go.

Then she concluded in capital letters: "SIN, YOU HAVE LOST!"

Of course there are times and periods of depression and gloom. Sometimes life grows dark; we get in a tunnel. When we get into a railway tunnel and it gets dark, what do we do? Throw away our ticket and jump off? No, we trust the engineer and hold on to our ticket! Having entered more than one tunnel of darkness in life, I have learned that there is wisdom in the words "This Too Shall Pass."

This is possible because we know to whom we belong — our God. Very early in life I had learned that the answer to the question, "What is your only comfort in life and death?" was:

> That I with body and soul, both in life and death, am not my own, but belong unto my faithful Saviour Jesus Christ, who, with his precious blood, have fully satisfied for all my sins, and delivered me from all the power of the devil; and so preserves me that without the will of my heavenly Father, not a hair can fall from my head; yea, that all things must be subservient to my salvation; and therefore, by His Holy Spirit, he also assures me of eternal life, and makes me sincerely willing and ready henceforth, to live with him.

(Heidelberg Catechism)

However, the real and final answer to the question of suffering lies beyond this present time. "I reckon that the sufferings of this present time are not worthy to be compared with the glory which shall be revealed in us" (Rom. 8:18).

Henry W. Frost of the China Inland Mission tells of a man who made clocks. One day he showed one of his clocks to a man who had never seen a clock before. Mr. Frost wrote this of the experience. "The fashioner of the clock opened the back of it and asked the man what he thought of its maker. The man saw some wheels, and other smaller ones, some going one way and others another way, some wheels slow and others fast. Seeing this seeming confusion he said, 'I think the man who made that is mad.' Then the maker took his friend to the front side of the clock and asked what he thought of its maker. The man looked at the two hands of the clock moving smoothly and regularly, each one in its appointed circle, and both of them telling perfectly the time of day, and then he said, 'I think the man who made that is the wisest person who ever lived.' "

And life does often seem like the wrong side of a clock. That is the way life seemed just after I entered the ministry. Three years previously I had left my lucrative position with Eastern Air Lines to attend Western Theological Seminary. Three years later, within weeks after graduation, all three of our children were in the hospital with polio. But I shall never forget the moment or the spot in the old parsonage of the First Reformed Church of Grand Haven, Michigan, where I knelt in prayer and said, "Lord, I surely don't understand, but you do — I hand it over to you." In that surrender God gave me peace. To me it looked like the wrong side of a clock, but the clockmaker was there making the wheels of circumstance keep the time of His perfect will.

After Danny had been ill about one year, he was again on the particular drug which caused considerable obesity. Whether it was this or a general deterioration caused by the disease, I don't know, but he was finding increasing difficulty in walking and moving about. His cheeks puffed out, there was a rather grotesque protruding of his stomach, and his ill-shaped body moved with the ungainly gait of a newborn colt. From a father's point of view it was pathetic.

The temptation to indulge in the sin of self-pity was always around. I think that Jesus actually faced this same temptation. It came when Peter suggested to Him that the Cross was unnecessary (Matt. 16:21-24). This temptation to self-pity followed these lines of reason: (1) Why must death come to one so young? (2) Why must death come to one so perfect? (3) Why must more hardship come to one who already had so much? Such questions were temptations to self-pity for Jesus. He overcame all such with the words, "Get thee behind me, Satan!" And in Hebrews we read that "for the *joy* that was set before him, he endured the cross, despising the shame."

Now, how does one avoid the sin of self-pity? Jesus said, "If any man will come after me, *let him deny himself,* take up his cross, and follow me." Self-pity is just the opposite of this formula; self-pity puts self squarely in the middle of life. Self-pity says, "My sorrow must have its due consideration; my situation has claim to everybody's pity and love." Self-pity is selfish and self-centered. And the only cure is to nail that self on Calvary's cross.

What a tragedy to become an addict to self-pity! "You don't deserve such treatment!" Peter told Jesus. Others may say that to us, or we may say it to ourselves. It is the voice of Satan, and he must be rebuked in Jesus' name.

The thought of Danny's leaving us was persistent. I was conscious of references to this subject in my reading. One day while reading a biography of Saint Francis of Assisi, I came upon the dying words of Clare, the first woman of the Franciscan Order. She had used them to comfort her own soul, and they now comforted mine. Communing with her own soul she spoke softly just before she died, "Go forth, Christian soul, go forth without fear, for thou hast a good Guide for thy journey. Go forth without fear, for He that created thee hath sanctified thee, always hath He protected thee, and He hath loved thee with the love of a mother."

This was the way we would want Danny to go, ". . . without fear, for thou hast a good Guide for thy journey."

Should we keep working hard at keeping Danny alive? An affirmative answer seemed obvious, and yet I couldn't help debating this question in my mind. There were times when it seemed it would be "right" just to let death take its victim, rather than prolong the struggle.

Danny lost his ability to walk, and he was very sensitive. Whenever I picked him up he would wince and shudder. Otherwise he was still comfortable and enjoyed life. The doctor had suggested that perhaps he should be hospitalized for a series of tests. We were opposed to this because Danny enjoyed being home so much with the family. While coloring, watching TV, or playing, it was extremely satisfying to him to have one of us near. He would pat our arms, smile at us, or spontaneously kiss us to show his contentment. We were glad his possible hospitalization at this time did not need to be carried out.

One day I expressed my feelings concerning this to our doctor. I said, "Doctor, as the drugs begin to lose their effectiveness, I hope we will let nature take its course and not try to drag life on after it becomes a heavy burden for Danny. It doesn't seem right," I went on, "to force his body to retain life when it is no longer fit to perform its function as a residence for the soul." Dr. Brubaker agreed with me and told me that they felt an obligation to continue the fight as long as they were meeting with some success, but that when the tide turned decisively against them, their work would then become that of making Danny as comfortable as possible.

My own secret prayer was that God would quietly and easily take Danny's life from him. I even dared pray that He would do it soon, or that Danny's mobility might return. I don't mean that I was giving God an ultimatum, but for Danny's sake it seemed to me that either God should have him now or, if he were to be with us, he should be allowed the use of his legs and have his bones lose the sensitiveness which made him wince and shudder whenever I picked him up.

I wish I could describe the dauntless, buoyant spirit Danny displayed throught all of this. I wish even more that others of us could capture that same spirit. I wondered what the secret source of his effervescent happiness could be? How could one who couldn't move six feet without being carried and whose bones ached at the slightest touch and who had to regularly undergo the minor surgery involved in a bone-marrow test without an anesthesia — how could such a one possibly greet the world with a blithe spirit? One answer was that these little ones do not doubt the care of God, even though they do not know the theological clichés we adults use. And I am sure they do not borrow the potential trouble of future days.

Danny's body became sorer, and it was increasingly difficult for him to be comfortable. On Veteran's Day we took the family for a picnic to an isolated roadside picnic area in Bouquet Canyon. Danny enjoyed the day with the children, even though he had to be carried around. His only request was, "When I stop being sore, will you take me here again?"

His delightful humor shone through his distress. On the way home he got a big thrill when we were pulled over to the side of the road by a motorcycle officer for "going forty-five in a thirty-five mile zone." That evening at the table Danny indicated he would be telling his friends about our encounter with the law. I suggested it might be better if he didn't say anything about it. "But listen, dad," he continued with a mischievous grin, "you tell people things I do and say."

Then came our evening devotions. Our Bible lesson was the story of the spying out of the Promised Land by Joshua, Caleb, and the other ten men and their encounter with the giants of Palestine. As usual Danny had questions. His first was, "Is God bigger than the giants?" Danny was thinking of physical bigness. Nevertheless, he had identified the whole point of the story. There were ten spies who figured the giants were bigger. There were two who figured God was bigger. It was a good opportunity to make a point about God's "bigness." His next question had no particular theological significance, yet it was interesting. After hearing that God was bigger than giants, he wanted to know, "Just what does God eat, anyway?"

During the time of Danny's illness a young Christian businessman, Jack Heck, became a member of our church. Jack had lost a seven-year-old daughter with leukemia. In his conversation with me concerning the illness and death of his daughter, Shirley, he told me something which proved to be a great help.

On the night of her death, Shirley was sleeping in her room. Jack heard her call to be taken to the bathroom, an experience with which we were very familiar. When she returned she said, "Daddy, there is a man standing at the foot of my bed." "It's me, honey," Jack said. "No, daddy," she said, "I see you, but this is a different man." I had always been hesitant about receiving this kind of story at face value. And yet how can it be explained, except to say it happened? If it was an older person who had been thinking and praying to Christ all his life, some would say it was a hallucination. But that would hardly explain this. At this time Jack was not a Christian, and the little girl had never been taught that Christ comes for His children at time of death. The girl had attended Sunday school but had no other religious training. The girl was completely conscious at the time and just as she told her daddy what she saw, her head sagged backward. Jack put his ear to her chest and heard the last faint beats of her heart. Well, what is so impossible about God making Himself known in this way at the closing moments of a little girl's life? I had always believed that when life is terminated the journey from "here" to "there" is not made alone. There was One waiting to escort, like the crossing guard who takes the children across the busy street on their way to school. The psalmist said, "Yea, though I walk through the valley of the shadow of death, I will fear no evil: for thou art with me" (Ps. 23:4).

Then I asked him, "Tell me, Jack, how long does it take for time to relieve the intense sorrow and heartache?" As at several other times God had had just the right answer at just the right time for me, Jack's answer was straightforward and unhesitant.

"Reverend Brunsting," he said, "death came as a real relief. It was as if a huge burden had been lifted. You see," he continued, "the heartache comes primarily from knowing that the child is uncomfortable and must face the difficulties which may be involved with death. Then when the apprehensions concerning death are passed and death itself has actually come, there comes a welcome easement."

Our old enemy, death, did not seem as formidable after that conversation. For Danny, who was our chief concern, death would mean that his Friend, Jesus, would come to bring an end to the misery of his diseased body and take our Danny and His Danny to His wonderful home. Death was, when needed, a welcome friend.

With that preparation of mind and heart for death, there remained just one more thing to do, and that was to arrange for the actual service. Alice and I had thought and talked about this matter for some time. Now we crystallized our thinking and took such action as was necessary.

First of all, we decided that the memorial service for Danny would be held in our church. I personally felt that funeral services should be held in churches rather than in places of business. We decided to ask our friend and neighbor, Lloyd Menning, to conduct the service and a friend of more than twenty years, Ed Hibma, to preach the sermon. Members of the church board would act as pallbearers. We also decided that since our residence in California would not necessarily be permanent, we would have the body taken to my hometown for interment.

Our next act was to see a local mortician to make the necessary arrangements and select the casket. We felt we were better qualified emotionally to do this before his death than to wait until Danny had passed away.

With this done, all our necessary preparation was finished.

On Thursday morning, the week before Thanksgiving, Danny went to see his doctor for a checkup. It was his last one. The doctor told us there was no use fighting any longer. Danny was taken off all the anti-cancer drugs.

Alice and I decided to keep him at home as long as possible. He would be much happier and could receive more attention at home than in a hospital.

After Danny stopped taking the powerful drugs, he seemed to feel better. He began to take a few bites of food and no longer had seizures of nausea. He entered into some of the games and conversation, watched TV, and on occasion sat at the table with us.

One evening after the meal, I asked Danny if he would like to say the prayer. Our Bible story had been about the brazen serpent. After thanking God for several things, he said, "And thank you there was a brass snake, so the people could look at it and their aches and pains would be gone." Then after a thoughtful pause he added, "Sure wish we could have a brass snake, too. Amen."

As Danny's life neared its end, I tried to think clearly through the reason for his life. Surely every life has a purpose, even one of five years' length.

Two facts bearing on this question are found in Isaiah 43:7. First, man is the product of the thought and activity of God. In this verse of Scripture three different words are used to state this. God said, "I created," which has reference to the original thought and action of God. Then, "I formed," which refers to all the processes of development. And finally, "I made," which speaks of the finality of the finished work. Danny was God's thought and God's creation.

When Jesus was before Pilate, He said, "To this end have I been born, and to this end am I come into the world, that I should bear witness unto the truth." For Danny, too, there was an "end," a "purpose." The same is true for everyone. The trouble is that many do not find out for what they were born or for what purpose they came into the world.

There is a day of birth, there is a day of death — but for many the significance of the interim is unknown.

In Isaiah 43:7 there is a second great fact which gives the answer — "for the glory of God." Any life which has accomplished that has justified its existence and fulfilled God's purpose for this life.

Did Danny's life glorify God? I think it did.

One parishioner also thought so and expressed herself in this note to me:

> Little Danny is as much a minister of the gospel as you or your father before you . . . unschooled, however, in theological studies, unordained by ecclesiastical formalities, but most certainly called by God to bring the love of Jesus to this hallowed spot in the valley. The beauty of the white spire reaching heavenward from its nest to God's greenery is merely an earthly symbol of the beauty of Christ's love overflowing from the hearts of the people within. For each one knows, in his or her own way, that little Danny has led us to a closer walk with God.

Danny had prayed for a "brass snake," but his aches and pains persisted until he was willing to take the pills in the bottle marked, "Take one every four hours for severe pain." The first time he tried to take one (he was an expert pill-taker after a year of practice), he couldn't get it down. It was extra large. He got a taste of it, which was very bitter, and from that time on he refused them. After nearly a week during which he was feeling quite miserable, he finally consented to try again. This time it went down and within an hour he was feeling better than he had for a long, long time. I could pick him up without a cry of pain, and he could sleep for hours at night without moaning. How thankful we were for this pain reliever. It is difficult to describe how much better we all felt when we knew that Danny's way was easier. How closely our spirits are bound to the lives of others! I know that my own spirit rose and fell from lightheartedness to despondency almost in exact parallel to Danny's physical well-being.

Another thought came to me. Many, many friends were praying with us for the easement of Danny's discomfort, and yet he was increasingly miserable. Then a small pill does in matter of minutes what prayer did not do in weeks. Some might be tempted to assume that medical science is a greater benefactor than God. But my understanding of the truth is that all healing and help is of God and that His usual mode of operation is by use of means such as physicians, medication, etc. Danny's relief did not come from a pill; it came from God through the use of a pill.

Why do some expect God to work differently here than we expect Him to work in any other area of life? The farmer knows he must plant, cultivate, and harvest his fields if he is to have a crop. And when it is time to eat, God feeds us through the work and labor of the farmer, the processor, and the housewife. We do not sit at the table and expect the food to fly down from heaven as the manna did. It could! But God's usual method is through earthly means.

I certainly believed, too, that God could bring direct relief to Danny, even heal him. In fact, until the day Danny died I prayed for his healing. Prayed with faith, too, that He could and that He would if it would conform to His purpose and His will.

No, that little pill wasn't doing something God couldn't do. It, like doctors, nurses, hospitals, and all of the healing profession, was an instrument of God's help.

It seems to me that there are two extremes to avoid. One is thinking that God achieves His purposes without natural laws. The other is thinking that God is excluded from a closed system of materialistic determinism. I agree with the carved inscription found over the archway of a French medical school: "I dressed his wounds, God healed him."

Mingled with our tears were many precious moments of happiness. One such experience occurred on Sunday night after the evening service when I was putting Danny to bed. We prayed together. First Danny prayed. He always began his prayers by saying, "Thank you, Jesus died on the Cross for our sins." Then he thanked the Lord that "we could go to church today." He said "we" although he didn't go himself. Then he prayed that he might get better. When it was my turn, I prayed, among other things, that we might all have a good night of sleep. When I finished, Danny said, "You know I always sleep good at night. You know why, daddy?" "No," I said, "why don't you tell me." "Well," Danny replied, "when I'm in bed I think of all the nice things that happened to me during the day and then I sleep good." I thought his anti-insomnia formula was a good one.

On the last day of November, Danny asked me to take him Christmas shopping. He wanted to get each member of the family a gift. "I'll hide them in the closet," he said. "Then they'll never find them, eh, dad?" My mind went back to the previous Christmas when we had begun our bout with death. Danny had been so happy then as we wrapped the New Testaments for all the men working on the new church, so that, as Danny put it, "they can know Jesus, too."

We wondered how this Christmas would be. Would Danny be with us?

The pressure and apprehension of waiting was not easy. We had to constantly school ourselves to heed the instruction of Christ: "Therefore do not be anxious about tomorrow, for tomorrow will be anxious for itself. Let the day's own trouble be sufficient for the day."

Chapter 6

Death had been our ever-present enemy for over a year. We had fought our enemy with all the weapons available in the arsenal of medical science. We had earnestly prayed to God to halt our enemy in its tracks. But it was pressing closer and closer.

In Revelation 6:8 this persistent foe, "Death," is described as riding "a pale horse." The Greek for pale (or livid) is *chloros,* from which comes the name of the greenish poison gas, chlorine. The ghastly horse, the color of a corpse, was the most horrible of the four horsemen of the apocalypse. So he had made himself known to us. He had caused us untold anguish of heart.

But in the closing days of Danny's life, we began to see death differently. I thought of the words of Thomas Fuller in the *Life of Monica:* "Drawing near her death, . . . her soul saw a glimpse of happiness through the chinks of her sickness-broken body."

Death began to appear as our benefactor. It would end Danny's physical discomfort, and it was a harbinger of heaven. I appreciated more fully the lines of Coleridge in "Epitaph on an Infant":

> *Death came with friendly care;*
> *The opening Bud to Heaven convey'd*
> *And bade it blossom there.*

Alice and I shared these beautiful words expressing so exactly our desire and faith. We were ready for death; we prayed for its coming. Death was no longer the horrible enemy but a much-wanted friend.

Danny was no longer enjoying this life — thank God there was an exit! Danny could only feebly and painfully participate in this life — thank God there was another Life!

Gradually the moorings to this life loosened. Danny was becoming more and more insensitive to his surroundings. Very little captured his interest any longer. Soon, we knew, he would be leaving us.

But would he? Would it really be a "leaving"? Not if we believe in the Catholic Church. I use the term in its true sense, the Universal Church, which does not include merely the fellowship of the saints who are in the church on earth, but the communion of all saints who have entered into rest and are beyond the vision of the senses.

The communion abides. We are not divided. We are waiting, and so are they. We are not perfected, and neither are they. So we are united in our waiting. We cannot visit them. I do not know whether they can watch us. I do not think so, except perchance now and then by some special permission of heaven.

These things are spoken of in a remarkable sermon, "Death Abolished," in which Dr. G. Campbell Morgan speaks of his experience and feeling at the time of the passing of his daughter:

> I pass no day that I am not conscious of the nearness of at least one who entered within the veil sixteen years ago, my first lassie; but I never try to bring her up to mutter to me. I never insult the high and holy revelation of God by making use of some fleshly medium that I may hear a whisper that is from hell and not from heaven. But I know the touch of her spirit upon mine, for the spirit life cannot be measured by the dimensions of the material. I know though she cannot come to me, I shall go to her.

Then he quotes these beautiful words:

> *Not as a child shall we again behold her;*
> *For when with raptures wild*
> *In our embraces we again enfold her,*
> *She will not be a child;*
> *But a fair maiden in her Father's mansion,*
> *Clothed in celestial grace;*
> *And beautiful with all the soul's expansion*
> *Shall we behold her face.*

Then Dr. Morgan closes the thought with a powerful sentence which I have pondered and from which I have drawn strength: "I have not lost my child; she is mine as she never was before."

Alice and I had decided that Danny would spend his last days at home with us. We knew he would like this better than being in a hospital. Again and again he showed us and told us that he was glad he was with us. "Stay with me," he would say. The slight moaning arising through his seeming unconsciousness would cease as we sat with him and stroked his arm. Besides the advantage for Danny, we had the satisfaction of knowing we were personally doing all we could for him. Of some significance, too, in making this decision were the hospital costs. In our particular case it was a decision we never regretted.

I had talked the situation over with my consistory, and they agreed it would be all right to spend what time was needed at home with Danny. The church had in operation an effective program of lay visitation. I limited my calling and counseling to a minimum and spent the rest of the time at home, where I did my studying and sermon preparation. I became Danny's nurse. He was too heavy for Alice to handle with assurance, and Danny realized this and insisted that I care for him. Many sermons, prayer meeting talks, and church duties were prepared with his labored breathing in my ear.

This, too, was an experience of God's grace in answer to many prayers. During these weeks I did not miss a single service. I felt the power and work of the Holy Spirit in a special way for my work. Also I was careful not to bring any grief or gloom into the pulpit. In fact, I felt and expressed the triumph and exhilaration of the Christian faith in a more definite way than I had known before. My caring for Danny left Alice free to care for the needs of the house and the other children. We did not want this to be a morbid experience for them, and it wasn't. Special outings and enjoyments were planned for them. The two older children were cognizant of all the implications of Danny's condition, and their understanding and unity with Alice and me was beautiful and inspiring. Their hearts knew a tenderness and comprehension usually seen only in adults.

Perhaps more than anything else our encounter with death was a school of prayer. My too careless, slipshod, and easygoing habits of prayer had come under the scrutiny and self-criticism aroused by a bitter experience.

One thing I had learned was in connection with the five specific requests I made of the Lord, not one of which was granted. First, before the diagnosis I had prayed that Danny's illness might not be fatal. Second, when I knew what was wrong, I prayed that a cure or control for leukemia might be found in time for Danny. Third, I prayed that if God was to take Danny that it would not be a long, drawn-out matter. Fourth, I prayed he might be healed. And fifth, after he was taken off all drugs, I prayed that his death might come quickly. As I say, not one of these five requests was granted as I prayed. But I did not feel my prayers were a failure. Prayer is not an opportunity for God to learn our will, but an opportunity for us to learn God's will. And God's will was made abundantly clear to me. As a testimony to God's goodness and grace I want to set it down here.

First of all, God had a purpose and meaning for Danny's life which, I trust, is shown in these pages. Second, God had a sustaining grace for us, Danny's parents, which allowed us — with joy! — to carry on our work and responsibilities in the home and church. And, third, it brought us into an intimacy with the Lord that we had never known before. This was better than what I had asked for.

During the morning of the day Danny died, which was Monday, December 14, 1959, he had alternate periods of quiet and restlessness. We sat with him and gave him every assistance possible. At one time it seemed he tried to communicate with us, but we were unable to understand what he said. He repeated the same thing three times, but the whole sentence was unintelligible to us except for one word which was heard distinctly each time. It was the word "home." I wonder what was in his mind? I knew he was much more satisfied being home than he could possibly have been in a hospital. Was this what he was thinking of? Or did this last word we heard him speak reveal that he knew something of another "home" to which he was going?

About noon Danny became very quiet, and for four hours he never moved, except for the rising and falling of his chest in shallow breathing. Then, shortly after four o'clock in the afternoon, his eyes opened in the blank stare of death, his teeth clenched, and as I held his head in my arm, his breathing stopped.

What happened in that solemn moment was well expressed in a telegram we later received from Dr. and Mrs. John R. Mulder: "God has spoken. You now have a treasure in heaven."

Immediately there came to our side the help, sympathy, and friendship of our beloved friends and relatives. Grief and sorrow must, in a sense, be borne alone, and yet in another real sense it can be divided so that each takes a little. There were so many who helped by "taking a little." What a comfort and strength to have Christian friends and dear relatives through whom God can channel His grace and love to us. Our pain was great; His grace and love were greater. God let our pain and sorrow be cushioned by a wonderful peace and calmness of heart.

The morning of the funeral service began with Alice and me reading from God's precious word and praying together. Then our three friends, Lloyd Menning, Herman Rosenberg, and John Hibma, conducted a simple but beautiful service.

I would like to include here the touching prayer offered by Reverend Rosenberg, hoping it may be a blessing to others as it certainly was to us:

Eternal and Everlasting God, Thou art our loving Father, our Blessed Redeemer and our Gracious Comforter. In this hour of sorrow we come into Thy presence in the Name of Jesus, our Savior.

We come with praise and devotion. Thy people have always praised Thee — even in the midst of sore trial. We would make an altar of our grief and tears and from this altar praise Thy Name, Oh Thou who art blessed forever. "Praise God from whom all blessings flow; Praise Him all creatures here below; Praise Him above, ye heavenly host; Praise Father, Son and Holy Ghost! Amen."

We come to Thee with contrition. We are a sinful people in need of forgiveness. We are troubled by Thy wrath. Oh, consume us not in thine anger. Our present sorrow does not give us entrance into the holy place of Thy presence. We come in the name of our Savior, Jesus Christ, who suffered the anguish of hell, the plagues of death, and the wrath of God for our redemption. Merciful Father, on the merit of His atoning sacrifice, forgive us and through the blood of His everlasting covenant cleanse us. With His righteousness clothe us and with His Spirit renew and heal us. With His promises enrich us and with His presence cheer us.

We come into Thy presence with thanksgiving. This for us is a day of drought and poverty because death has removed a loved one from us. Our hearts are heavy and sad. We feel as though the words of the ancient prophet describe our day. "Although the fig tree shall not blossom, neither shall fruit be in the vine; the labour of the olive shall fail, and the fields shall yield no meat; the flock shall be cut off from the fold, and there shall be no herd in the stall."

The blossom of a boyish smile is gone. The fruit of a boyish laughter is no more. The activity of busy boyish hands has ceased. But with the ancient prophet our hearts rejoice in Thee, and we joy in the God of our salvation. In this season, as in every season, we thank Thee for Him who though He was rich yet for our sakes became poor that we through His poverty might become rich. We thank Thee that we are forgiven, that we are reconciled, that our names are written in the Lamb's book of life, that we have hope which is as an anchor to our souls, that we have the Holy Ghost to comfort us and guide us through this earthly pilgrimage to the City of Light, and that we have thine own dear presence, precious Savior. We pray Thee to fashion our hands and empower our arms to embrace Thee and energize our hearts to love Thee. The world has never meant less, and Thou hast never meant more. In Thy light we see light. Death holds no terror. The grave has been sanctified. Parting is but for a moment. From grateful thankful hearts we sing, "Bless the Lord, O my soul, and all that is within me bless His holy name. Bless the Lord, O my soul, and forget not all His benefits."

We thank Thee particularly for little Danny. In wisdom and mercy Thy hand fashioned his body, mind, and soul. We thank Thee for all the qualities that Thou didst pour into his life which made his person so dear and precious. We thank Thee for Thy grace which allowed him to live in this lovely family bond these four years. We thank Thee for sending him into a home in which the forbearers for generations have been sealed in the covenant. We thank Thee that these parents claimed the promises of this covenant and that we know that their little lamb is in Thy bosom. We thank Thee for this precious family: for Bernard, Alice, Bernie, Al, Carol, and Dorothy whom Thou in Thy infinite wisdom didst choose to love and cherish little Danny in sickness and in health. We thank Thee also for this fatal illness which has bound us to this family and to Thee. We do not presume to understand, but we bow before the majesty of Thy sovereign will and pray, "The Lord gave and the Lord hath taken away; blessed be the name of the Lord."

We come to Thee with our supplications. Hear us as we pray for those who are lost in the night of sin. Make our hearts tender and lay these souls upon our hearts. Thou hast called us as ministers and laymen to declare Thy truth to these masses mingling in the darkness. Thou hast called us to preach and teach the Gospel to this generation on whom we feel the end of the age has come. Wipe the tears from our eyes. Put the power of Thy Holy Spirit in our frail bodies, minds, and wills. Help us to lift the trumpet of the Gospel to our lips and declare to all the world that Jesus saves.

We come to Thee to commit this beloved family into Thy care. We pray for them as we pray for ourselves:

"There is a safe and secret place beneath the
 wings divine,
Reserved for all the heirs of grace; O be that
 refuge mine.

The least and feeblest there may bide uninjured
 and unawed;
While thousands fall on every side, He rests
 secure in God.

He feeds in pastures large and fair of love and
 truth divine;
O child of God, O glory's heir, how rich a lot
 is thine.

A hand almighty to defend, an ear to every call,
An honored life, a peaceful end, and heaven to
 crown it all."

Amen

The next morning I left by plane with Danny's body for the service and burial in Sioux Center, Iowa. There on a cold Saturday morning we laid his little body to rest in a grave immediately adjacent to my father's.

The cards and letters and words and deeds from several hundred friends were helpful beyond measure. From one of these expressions of sympathy the following lines by Douglas Mallock seemed particularly appropriate and helpful.

Time cannot take our boy away;
Time cannot change him – all the years
Can never turn one hair to gray;
Can never turn one smile to tears.

As fair and boyish he appears
As on an unforgotten day
He dropped his toys, he left his play,
And slipped from earth, to all the spheres.

I often envied others when
I saw their sons, so fine and tall;
And then a memory came again
Of one small boy forever small.

Grief has this comfort after all,
Girls grow to women, boys to men,
But they are still the same as then,
The children that the grieved recall.

Having so many friends who shared our grief was like distributing a heavy load among many bearers, making the load lighter and easier for each.

I returned home from Iowa on Christmas Eve and was awakened early Christmas morning, as I had been every year since the children came, to see what each exciting package under the tree contained. With bursting expressions of delight and joy they were opened, and it was then that our life began to return to the normal stream and pattern of living — but now without Danny. Could life be "normal" without him, the one who had been the object of so much affection, attention, and concern — the source of so much joy and happiness? It would have to be! Time must move, and movement is change, and change must include death as well as birth; and life is held in time, and so the stream moves and moves until "time shall be no more." Yes, life would return to "normal," even though that "normal" would be different than it was before.

For others and outsiders, our family would now be numbered and thought of without Danny. For me, Danny would always be a part of the family. He wouldn't be eating with us; he wouldn't be sleeping in our house; we wouldn't see him going off for his first day of school. Yet somehow, some way, he would never leave our family. My feeling about Danny remaining a part of the family was put into words by William Wordsworth in a satisfying poem entitled "We Are Seven."

> *A simple child,*
> *That lightly draws its breath,*
> *And feels its life in every limb,*
> *What should it know of death?*
>
> *I met a little cottage girl;*
> *She was eight years old, she said;*
> *Her hair was thick with many a curl*
> *That clustered round her head.*
>
> *She had a rustic, woodland air,*
> *And she was wildly clad;*
> *Her eyes were fair, and very fair;*
> *–Her beauty made me glad.*
>
> *"Sisters and brothers, little maid,*
> *How many may you be?"*
> *"How many? Seven in all," she said,*
> *And wondering looked at me.*
>
> *"And where are they? I pray you tell."*
> *She answered, "Seven are we;*
> *And two of us at Conway dwell,*
> *And two are gone to sea.*

"Two of us in the churchyard lie,
  My sister and my brother;
And in the churchyard cottage I
  Dwell near them with my mother."

"You say that two at Conway dwell,
  And two are gone to sea,
Yet ye are seven! I pray you tell,
  Sweet maid, how this may be?"

Then did the little maid reply:
  "Seven boys and girls are we;
Two of us in the churchyard lie,
  Beneath the churchyard tree."

"You run about, my little maid,
  Your limbs they are alive;
If two are in the churchyard laid,
  Then ye are only five."

"Their graves are green, they may be seen,"
  The little maid replied,
"Twelve steps or more from my mother's door,
  And they are side by side.

"My stockings there I often knit,
  My kerchief there I hem;
And there upon the ground I sit,
  And sing a song to them.

"And often after sunset, sir,
  When it is light and fair,
I take my little porringer,
  And eat my supper there.

"The first that died was little Jane;
  In bed she moaning lay,
Till God released her of her pain;
  And then she went away.

"So in the churchyard she was laid;
  And when the grass was dry,
Together round her grave we play'd,
  My brother John and I.

"And when the ground was white with snow,
   And I could run and slide,
My brother John was forced to go,
   And he lies by her side."

"How many are you, then," said I,
   "If they two are in Heaven?"
The little maiden did reply,
   "Oh, master, we are seven!"

"But they are dead – those two are dead,
   Their spirits are in Heaven!"
'Twas throwing words away, for still
The little maid would have her will,
   And said, "Nay, we are seven!"

So it would be in our family. Danny would never be gone. A little fellow whom we wanted so much — a dear little fellow for whom we would have gone to the ends of the earth if it would have helped to keep him — was gone from his toys, from his bed, from the family table, but never gone from our hearts.

O God, how I wish I still had that little boy! Yet I do have him. I will always have him — in my heart where I also have Jesus. Danny and Jesus, my son and God's Son.